Planting Techniques

Planting Techniques

Jennifer Stackhouse
Debbie McDonald

MURDOCH BOOKS

Contents

Welcome

To say I've always gardened is probably a bit of a stretch, but I've certainly grown plants for as long as I can remember. My earliest memories are in gardens (I distinctly remember being on eye level with a foxglove at just 18 months of age) and my favourite moments have mostly revolved around a plant or a garden.

And the same goes for Debbie. We both agree that milestones in our lives somehow always seem to revolve around plants. We both had garden weddings, celebrate our birthdays and those of our children in gardens, and we both love to spend holidays visiting gardens. And it goes without saying we have created gardens wherever we have lived.

We know that our love of gardens and being in among plants with our hands in the soil comes from growing up in a family of gardeners—there is a strong genetic component for both of us. We trace that gardening gene back many generations in our respective families. Hopefully we've another generation of gardeners in the making following behind us (although my kids certainly seem to be more immersed in the business of growing up in our tech-savvy world than spending too much time with mum in the garden!).

Of course it is one thing to be interested in plants, it is taking it to another level to turn it into your day job, but that's what we have both ended up doing. We studied horticulture and then spent time working in gardens and nurseries before finally coming together on ABC *Gardening Australia* magazine. Writing this book, the second in our series of practical garden guides, has been a natural progression of our interest and our work. We are keen to share what we know about growing plants and a book seems a great way to do it.

Once you start to look at plants with a view to growing them rather than just admiring them you start to wonder about all aspects of the plant and what makes it tick. When I see a plant—whether it's a tall tree or an annoying weed—I like to know what part of the world it comes from, what conditions it likes to grow in, when it flowers, how you feed and nurture it (or don't in the case of a weed). Through such observations you can learn how a particular plant might grow in your garden and what it needs to grow well.

Looking more closely at plants also leads you to talk plants to other keen gardeners, to read about plants and gardens, and to travel to other parts of the world to see plants growing in their natural habitats.

However, if you didn't grow up in a family of gardeners and then pursue plants and gardens as a career as Debbie and I have done, you may feel the need of some very practical advice. As it just isn't possible for us to pop around to your garden and help out (although that would be a great way to spend our time) we thought we'd pool our resources and turn them into a book that deals with the nitty gritty of actually growing a plant.

So that's what this book is all about. We take you from getting started with buying a plant and getting it into the ground, through to its day-to-day care. As well we look at the landmark events in any plant's life. We examine those times of repotting, pruning, fertilising and propagation. We also look at the tools you may need to get your garden growing and how to look after them.

With the best gardening techniques around however things still go wrong. Plants succumb to pests and diseases or languish if their growing conditions are not quite right. We've examined this side of gardening as well with hints about how to work out what to do when things aren't quite going to plan.

Although the topics covered in this book are the very nuts and bolts of gardening it is amazing at how little of this information is readily available and packaged up in a useful and accessible way. We hope through our words, photographs and the step-by-step details throughout this book you'll be able to grow plants better and also understand more about what makes them tick.

With this book too we've added a cheat sheet. Well, it is called a glossary, but it is really a great place to check all those terms that seem to grow along with plants. If you've wondered what something means we hopes you'll be able to find out quickly in this book. Then, with the confidence that comes with a bit of knowledge and the enthusiasm to get out there and grow, you'll be able to move into unchartered territory by propagating your own plants and even passing on your knowledge to others.

Perhaps this book should come with a warning—gardening is addictive. Once you start, you may not be able to stop. That's what we hope, anyway.

Happy gardening!

Jennifer Stackhouse and Debbie McDonald

CHAPTER 1

Getting started

Why do I need to read this chapter?

- To find out how to choose a good quality plant.
- To learn how to avoid a root-bound plant.
- To discover the best time to plant for optimum growth.

How to select a plant

Before you can actually plant anything at all in your garden it helps to know how to select and purchase plants at different times of the year.

The first step towards having a flourishing plant lies in choosing a good quality, healthy specimen from the nursery.

Whatever type of plant you are buying, ensure its size is in proportion to its pot, the leaves are green and vibrant, and it is rooted in the pot without being root-bound.

Avoid any pot with weeds and make sure it has no pests or diseases on board. Choose a plant with a good shape, no broken or oddly shaped branches or split trunks. If you are buying a tree, select one with a firm, undamaged trunk and strong growing shoot (or 'leader').

Select flowering plants with buds rather than fully open blooms for a longer blooming period.

Try to buy plants that have recently arrived in stock and avoid any that appear to have been there too long. Watch out for split or faded pots or labels, yellowing foliage or weeds in pots—these are all indicators that the plant has been too long in the nursery and may not be a good buy.

Finally, look for a bonus that gives extra value, such as growth that could provide good cutting material, or a clumping plant that could be divided.

If plants have been badly grown or badly cared for before you buy them, the chances are they will not grow well when you plant them. Be very wary of plants on the 'bargain' table.

Checklist for buying a quality plant

- Look for newly arrived stock
- Buy plants that look healthy and vigorous
- Select plants in proportion with their pots
- Don't take home pests, diseases or weeds
- Check for strong healthy roots
- Don't buy damaged or spindly plants
- Choose buds over flowers

Avoiding a root-bound plant

The key to buying a successful plant lies in the plant's roots. One indicator of potential problems is a plant that is root-bound (also called pot bound). This occurs when the plant's roots have completely filled their pot or container and have begun to circle and twist within the pot. This happens when the plant has been growing for too long in a container that is too small.

There are telltale signs that indicate a plant is root-bound before you

TOP A good quality plant will slip easily from the pot, ready to plant.
BOTTOM This daisy has outgrown its pot and so is not a good buy.
OPPOSITE LEFT A severely root-bound plant.
OPPOSITE RIGHT Coir fibre pots can be planted straight into the ground, pot and all.

examine the root system. If the plant looks too big for its container—particularly if it dries out quickly or is prone to blowing over—then it may be root-bound. A faded pot or faded, curled label may also indicate that a plant has been in the container for longer than is healthy and is likely to be root-bound.

The easiest way to discover whether a plant has a good root system is to examine it. Before the plant is purchased, lift or gently tip it out of its pot (this is also known as 'knocking' a plant out of its pot). If the plant is in a nursery, ask a member of the nursery staff to do this for you.

When a plant is root-bound, there's very little potting mix remaining and the roots are thick and tangled. In this condition the plant will have trouble establishing after planting. Don't buy it.

Plantable pots

Many plants are now available in biodegradable pots that can be planted straight into the ground. These are made of peat, recycled cardboard or cornstarch-based plastic. All these materials will break down in the soil, or when placed in the compost heap.

The chances of a plant becoming root-bound in this type of pot are minimised as the roots are able to grow through the pot. Being able to plant pot and plant together also means there is no risk of transplant shock, and no down-time while the plant recovers from being planted.

A word of caution: coir and peat pots can dry out very quickly, especially on hot or windy days or if the plants are exposed to the sun.

Cornstarch-based pots are not so prone to drying out. Once you get the plant home, ensure you water it every day and plant it as soon as possible. If it can't be planted immediately, place the coir or peat pot into a cover pot or recycled plastic or metal container.

If a plant has dried out in a recyclable or conventional pot, you can rehydrate it by soaking it in a bucket of water until bubbles stop rising from the potting mix. Small pots should be rehydrated in just 10 minutes or so but larger pots may take 30 minutes or more of soaking.

Once the plant, pot and its potting mix have been sufficiently revived, plant them into the garden or another container. Finish up by watering with care, ensuring the water provided soaks in to the rootball area.

ABOVE LEFT Rehydrate potted plants by soaking in a bucket of water. **ABOVE RIGHT** Dormant, leafless plants are a good buy in winter.

Planting times

Some plants are fussier than others about their planting times. Climatic conditions that affect planting include frost, extremes in temperature and the availability of soil moisture.

Planting at the optimum time is often crucial to the plant's survival. The best way to achieve this is by having an understanding of each plant's growth cycle and the nature of its growth. The ideal plant times are either during winter, when most plants are dormant or as a growth begins. The beginning of a plant's growth cycle is usually between spring and autumn, and this is the best time to plant.

Avoid planting in very hot or dry periods: the plant will suffer for it, and perhaps not survive. During a dormant period, plants are easier to handle and plant, and often a lot cheaper to buy.

Many ornamental and productive plants are dormant during winter.

It is during this period that winter deciduous plants, such as roses, are sold in a condition known as 'bare rooted'. This means that the plant's roots are removed from soil or potting mix, wrapped in coir peat, sphagnum moss or some other lightweight horticultural fibre medium, and contained in a plastic sleeve. Once planted, dormant plants often will not begin to grow until the soil and air conditions warm up and become favourable in spring.

Seasonal planting calendar

The following guide outlines the best planting times for a range of commonly grown garden plants. If you buy a plant that is growing in a pot, you can usually put it in the ground at any time, provided care is taken to protect it from extreme heat or cold. Plant frost-sensitive annuals and perennials after all threat of frost has passed.

Plant	Sold as	Season	Plant	Sold as	Season
Almond	bare rooted	Autumn to early spring	Dill	seed	Spring to summer
Alyssum	seed, seedling	Spring to autumn	Dutch iris	bulb	Autumn
Anemone	corm	Late summer to autumn	Eggplant	seed, seedling	Spring to summer
Apple	bare-rooted	Autumn to early spring	Eucomis	bulb	Winter to spring
Aquilegia	seed, seedling	Summer to autumn	Fennel	seed, seedling	Spring to autumn
Artichoke, globe	division, crown	Spring	Fig	bare rooted	Autumn to early spring
Artichoke, Jerusalem	tuber	Spring	Forget-me-not	seed	Spring
Asparagus	crown	Autumn to winter	Freesia	corm	Autumn
Basil, annual	seed, seedling	Spring to late summer	Garlic	bulb	Autumn to winter
Begonia, bedding	seed, seedling	Spring to early summer	Ginger	rhizome	Spring to autumn
Broccoli	seed, seedling	Autumn to winter	Hollyhock	seed, seedling	Late summer to spring
Calendula	seed, seedling	Spring, autumn	Hydrangea	bare-rooted	Winter to early spring
Capsicum	seed, seedling	Spring to late summer	Impatiens	seed, seedling	Spring to summer
Celery	seed, seedling	Spring	Iris	rhizome	Autumn to spring
Celosia	seed, seedling	Spring to late summer	Jonquil	bulb	Late summer to autumn
Cherry	bare rooted	Late autumn to early spring	Kniphofia	perennial	Spring to winter
Chilli	seed, seedling	Spring to late summer	Lavender	perennial	Autumn to spring
Chrysanthemum	perennial	Winter to spring	Lemon grass	seedling	Spring to summer
Cineraria	seed, seedling	Summer to autumn	Lilium	bulb	Autumn to spring
Coriander	seed	Spring to autumn	Linaria	seed	Summer to autumn
Cornflower	seed, seedling	Spring, autumn	Lobelia	seed, seedling	Spring to autumn
Crabapple	bare rooted	Autumn to early spring	Lotus	crown	Spring to summer
Crepe myrtle	bare rooted	Autumn to early spring	Lupin	seed, seedling	Spring, autumn
Cucumber	seed, seedling	Spring to summer	Lycoris	bulb	Winter to spring
Daffodil	bulb	Autumn	Marigold	seed, seedling	Spring to autumn
Dahlia	tuber	Spring to summer	Marjoram	seed, seedling	Spring to autumn
Delphinium	seed, seedling	Spring	Matthiola	seed, seedling	Autumn to early spring
Dianthus	seed, seedling	Spring	Mexican sunflower	seed, seedling	Spring to winter

▶

Plant	Sold as	Season
Nasturtium	seed, seedling	Any time
Nectarine	bare rooted	Late autumn to winter
Nerine	bulb	Winter to spring
Onion	bulb	Autumn to spring
Pansy	seed, seedling	Autumn to winter
Paper daisy	seed, seedling	Autumn
Parsley	seed, seedling	Any time
Parsnip	seed	Spring to autumn
Peach	bare rooted	Late autumn to winter
Pear	bare rooted	Late autumn to winter
Peas	seed, seedling	Autumn to spring
Phlox	seed, seedling	Spring to summer
Phlox, perennial	crown	Winter to spring
Pineapple	off shoot, cutting	Spring to summer
Plum	bare rooted	Late autumn to winter
Poppy, Californian	seed	Spring to summer
Poppy, Iceland	seed, seedling	Autumn to winter
Portulaca	seed, seedling	Spring to summer
Potato*	tuber	Spring, autumn
Primula	seed, seedling	Late summer to autumn
Pumpkin	seed	Spring to early summer
Quince	bare rooted	Late autumn to winter
Radish	seed	Spring to autumn
Ranunculus	bulb	Autumn
Raspberry	bare rooted	Late autumn to winter
Rhubarb	crown	Winter
Rhubarb	seedling	Spring to summer
Rocket	seed	Any time
Rose	bare rooted	Late autumn to winter

Plant	Sold as	Season
Rudbeckia	perennial	Autumn to early spring
Salvia	perennial	Late autumn to early spring
Shasta daisy	perennial	Late autumn to early spring
Silver beet	seed, seedling	Autumn to spring
Snowdrop	bulb	Autumn
Snowflake	bulb	Autumn
Spinach, English	seed, seedling	Autumn to spring
Snow pea	seed, seedling	Autumn to spring
Spring onion	seed, seedling	Any time
Strawberry	runners	Summer to autumn
Strawberry*	virus-free seedling	Autumn to spring
Sunflower	seed	Late spring to summer
Sweet corn	seed	Late spring to summer
Sweet pea	seed	Autumn to spring
Sweet potato	tuber	Spring
Tarragon	seed	Spring
Tomato	seed, seedling	Late winter to early autumn
Torenia	seed, seedling	Spring to summer
Tulip	bulb	Autumn
Verbena	seed, seedling	Spring to summer
Vinca	seed, seedling	Spring to summer
Viola	seed, seedling	Autumn to winter
Wallflower	seed, seedling	Autumn to winter
Water lily	crown	Late winter to spring
Watermelon	seed	Spring to early summer
Windflower	perennial	Spring
Zinnia	seed, seedling	Spring to summer
Zucchini	seed, seedling	Spring to summer

* Some plants succumb to incurable viruses. To avoid these, look for virus-free options for strawberries and potatoes.

OPPOSITE Aquilegias flower in spring and are grown from seed or seedlings. They are biennial so will need a full growing season before flowering.

CHAPTER 2

Basic planting

Why do I need to read this chapter?

- To avoid making a $2 planting hole.

- To learn how to get potted plants into the ground or another container.

- To find out how to plant seedlings, bulbs, bare-rooted and grafted plants and keep them growing.

Avoiding a $2 hole

Getting plants into the ground is a fun part of gardening. Every plant you put into the soil or a container offers the promise of growth and transformation with foliage, flowers and perhaps even a crop to harvest. Plants also change their environment, providing shade, shelter or habitat. Some plants grow quickly and live for only a season, while others grow to maturity more slowly but live for decades if not centuries. Whatever they become, the journey begins with the planting.

There is a cliché in the gardening world that you never put a $10 plant in a $2 hole. In other words, if you don't spend money on the soil, there's no point spending money on the plant.

A $2 or 'cheap' hole would be either too deep or not deep enough for the rootball. It has no added organic matter, fertiliser or wetting agents.

In order to prepare the hole for the plant, dig the planting hole at least twice as wide as the rootball but only as deep. This means a plant that's being transferred from a 20 cm pot into the ground would require a planting hole

that's about 40 cm across and at least the depth of the pot. A larger pot needs a wider, but not necessarily deeper, hole.

If you are digging a hole into a garden bed, take care that you don't disturb any nearby plants and their roots or any dormant bulbs or rhizomes. If there is a chance there are plants in the area where you are digging, it's a good idea to use a small trowel or small spade to dig, and proceed carefully. Also watch out for buried irrigation lines or pipes.

A word about soil

In heavy or clay-based soils, it's important to ensure the soil drains well. To check drainage, dig a hole approximately the same depth as your planting hole will be, fill it with water, and see how long it takes for the water to drain. The water should drain within several hours. If not, improve the soil.

LEFT Dig a hole that's wider but no deeper than the rootball you are planting.

The higher the clay component of the soil, the more slowly water drains away. In a very dense clay soil water may remain in the planting hole the next day or longer. If the hole has poor drainage, your plant's roots will be waterlogged, which has a detrimental effect on your plant's health. Root dieback, root disease or even plant death could result.

It is possible to improve the soil's drainage, even for soil with a high clay component. Planting in a raised bed may be a better approach in gardens with heavy or poorly draining soils.

In sandy or loamy soil, water drains much more quickly than it would from a heavy clay soil.

If you add water to a hole dug in sandy or loamy soil, the water will often be drained completely within an hour of being added. This can cause its own problems. If the water drains away quickly, plants can't absorb it fast enough, leading to root dieback and even plant death.

If your soil can benefit from added nutrients and compost—and most soils will—the time to add them is with your new plant, or in the preceding weeks. The best option is to improve the soil prior to planting, allowing two weeks or more between digging in fertiliser, manure or compost and planting. This allows the added organic matter or fertiliser to become incorporated into the existing soil.

Alternatively, use slow-release fertiliser pellets when planting as this

Tip Where you are adding a lot of manure or fertiliser to the soil at planting, take care to place soil between the enriched soil and the root system to avoid root burn or root death.

ABOVE Lining a planting hole with several sheets of newspaper will slow water loss in well-drained soil.

keeps fertiliser out of direct contact with roots.

There are two ways to incorporate organic matter into the soil. One is to add organic matter to the planting hole. This raises the soil level, and assists with drainage. If you don't want to raise the soil level, remove some of the improved soil to use elsewhere. This keeps the soil at its original level.

Tip If your soil is very sandy, try lining the planting hole with a layer of newspaper. This will slow the rate at which water drains from the hole, allowing it to be taken up by the plant's new root system. Eventually the newspaper rots, by which time the root system should have grown and the plant adapted to its new, well-drained situation.

Step-by-Step

HOW TO PLANT A PLANT

1 Dig a hole and mix plenty of compost or manure into the planting soil.

2 Knock the plant out of its pot. To do this, support the plant in one hand, upend the pot and firmly tap the bottom. The pot should slide off.

3 Place the plant in the hole, making sure that the top of the potting mix is at the same level as the surface of the ground. Backfill around the plant with the soil that was dug out of the hole and firm down.

4 Water well, and adjust any irrigation lines so that the plant will receive water. Spread mulch around the plant, and water again.

The second method is to shovel the soil out of the hole, then add organic matter and fertiliser, such as blood and bone, to the soil before replacing it around the plant. To keep the lawn or surroundings free of earth when you remove the soil, use a ground sheet or wheelbarrow to mix the soil and compost.

Round or square?

Some people believe that planting holes should be round to match the shape of the rootball. Not everyone agrees, with others claiming that a square hole encourages better, stronger root growth.

The truth is, neither of these theories about round or square holes appear to be supported by scientific evidence. So long as the hole you dig can accommodate the rootball, the shape of the hole appears to have very little long-term effect on the development of the plant.

So, what's the bottom line? Quite simply, you can dig whatever shape hole you like!

Warning!

When planting, look for pests and weeds. Examine the root system for insects or air pockets that can hinder future growth. Ants, slugs, snails or curl grubs can all take up residence in a plant's root system. Weeds may also be growing, so remove these including roots, bulbs or corms.

Some extra tips to give your plant the best start

Make sure the roots are watered well before planting. To do this, soak the plant in a bucket of water or water it thoroughly before planting.

Check the roots. Tease out roots that are tangled or twisted, pruning away any that are densely matted or damaged. Remove any damaged roots.

Avoid air pockets. Backfill around the rootball, pressing it down firmly as you go. Watering while planting will also help to remove air pockets.

Remove the plant label and tie. Don't leave it on the plant as it can damage the stem or branch it is tied to. Over time it also fades so there will be no record of the plant's name. For a lasting record, store the label in a planting book or container.

Slow-release or controlled-release fertiliser prills are easy to apply. They are a good option when you wish to avoid having raw fertiliser or other nutrients in direct contact with roots or foliage. After planting apply slow-release fertiliser over the surface and top off with a layer of mulch. This also helps to remove air pockets.

Step-by-Step

DIGGING A HOLE INTO LAWN

1 Start off by removing the turf. To do this, mark out the size of the planting hole then use a sharp spade to dig through and under the turf.

2 Slide the spade under the turf and lift or roll up the entire piece of grass. You may need to cut the piece of turf into sections (sods) to make lifting and removal easier.

3 Dig the area over removing any remaining roots, breaking up clods and getting rid of stones and rocks.

4 In most cases the planting soil benefits from the addition of organic matter at this stage.

5 The next stage is to dig the planting hole. To keep your lawn soil-free, place the soil from the hole onto a ground sheet or into a wheelbarrow.

6 Place the plant into the hole and fill with soil, firming the soil down around the plant. Water, mulch and water again.

1

2

3

4

5

6

Tip Waste not, want not! The section of turf that was removed can be used to fill bare patches elsewhere in the lawn or to start a new area of lawn by breaking it into sprigs or rooted cuttings for replanting.

Planting into lawn

If you are digging a hole into lawn or a rough uncultivated area where there are no nearby plants, you need to prepare the area differently than you would if you were planting into a garden bed. As lawn grass can quickly engulf a new plant and also rob the young plant of both water and nutrients, you will need to remove a large area of grass from where the new plant is to grow. Aim to remove at least enough lawn to leave the space clear where the potential root system is to grow. For a tree, this could be up to 2 m or so around the planting site.

After planting, cover this area with some type of mulch, in order to keep weeds and regrowth away. If you are planting into a lawn that is made up of a running grass that spreads by rhizomes (such as couch, kikuyu or buffalo) also install a root barrier or edging to keep the roots away from the plant. To create a root barrier, sink the edging to your garden bed into the soil, so the underground runners are prevented from entering the garden bed. Having a solid edging around a garden bed also makes mowing easier.

If you don't have a root barrier or don't create an edging, regularly clear the grass away by using a sharp spade to redig the edge of the bed.

Generally speaking, it is a better idea to dig a large garden bed to separate plants from the lawn than to make lots of small holes in a lawn for planting individual trees and shrubs.

Tip By removing grass from around a tree that you are planting, you also avoid the need to mow or trim close to the trunk, which can prove hazardous for the tree. It's important to note that lawns rarely thrive under the shade of a tree, just another reason to keep the area clear of grass.

Tip If you want to save your back, a no-dig way to kill grass before planting is to cover it with layers of newspaper, compost and mulch. Leave it for a few months and then plant straight into it through the mulch and newspaper layer. There may be some stray grass runners still hanging on, but these can be easily lifted with a fork and removed.

ABOVE When planting a feature tree in lawn, remove the turf in sods to use elsewhere.

Special techniques

Bulbs, small plants like seedlings, bare-rooted and grafted plants all need special planting techniques to get them off to the best start. Particular growing environments impact on the plant's growth, making alternative planting techniques preferable. Here are some tips for other planting methods.

Long-stem or deep planting

The various planting methods already explained in this chapter are traditional methods, whereby the stem of the plant isn't buried any more deeply in its new position than it was in its initial location. However, in recent years a new system of planting has been developed that completely turns traditional planting methods on their head. It has been developed by bush regenerators who have been able to demonstrate that for some plant species it is possible to plant the rootball and stem more deeply in the soil than the plant was growing in the pot. Depths vary between 20 and 100 cm. Not only does the plant grow, the extra root system that forms also means that the specimen outgrows those established by traditional methods.

This rapid growth occurs because the buried stem produces extra roots. The larger, stronger root system

OPPOSITE Deep planting techniques can help bush regenerators re-establish native plants.

Step-by-Step

DEEP PLANTING

1 Place the plant in a bucket of diluted seaweed tonic to ensure the potting mix is soaked through.

2 Dig a hole so that when the plant is placed in it, about two thirds of the stem will be underground.

3 Fill the hole with water and allow it to drain away. This ensures that the plant has adequate moisture while it gets established. With larger plants that are buried quite deeply, it can be worthwhile watering the soil every 10 cm or so as you're filling in the hole.

4 Remove foliage along the stem for the length that will be buried. Place the plant in the hole and backfill with soil, firming down as you go.

5 Water, mulch and water again.

provides the plant with faster access to soil moisture and nutrients. Deeper planting also gives the plant access to soil moisture at deep levels; insulates roots from extremes of heat and cold closer to the soil surface; and makes the plant more stable in the ground, reducing the need to stake new plants.

Not all plants are suitable for deep planting. Plants that grow from clumps or rhizomes may rot, and plants that are difficult to grow from cuttings may also fail to form roots along the stem, making them unsuitable to be planted in this manner.

Soil type also contributes to the success or failure of this new planting method. Soil that is poorly drained or has highly acidic or alkaline subsoil may not be suited for deep planting.

To try this method in your garden, experiment first by making some trial plantings at different depths.

Planting bulbs

Bulbs are planted when they are dormant. They need around three to six months to emerge from the ground, grow foliage and flower. This means late-winter and spring-flowering bulbs such as daffodil, tulip and bluebell are planted in late autumn for flowers in late winter to spring. Summer- to autumn-flowering bulbs are planted in late winter or early spring.

Most bulbs are planted pointy side up (the pointy end is generally where the shoot appears, while the roots appear from the broader base). The

Step-by-Step

HOW TO PLANT BULBS

1. Dig a hole with a spade or a trowel. Bulbs make the most impact in a garden planted in groups, so either dig individual holes close together, or dig one large hole where several bulbs will fit.

2. Place the bulbs in the hole, leaving a space that is the width of each bulb between them, with the pointy ends facing upwards.

3. Carefully cover the bulbs with the soil you dug out of the hole.

4. Cover with mulch and mark the position with a label. Water well.

Tip There's always an exception to every rule. Unlike other bulbs, spring-flowering anemones (*Anemone coronaria*) are planted pointy end down. This is because these chocolate drop-shaped corms produce root growth from the pointy part that looks like its shoot.

Step-by-Step

HOW TO PLANT BARE-ROOTED PLANTS

1 Remove the plastic bag and any packing material from around the roots of the plant. Soak the roots in a bucket of diluted seaweed tonic so they are well hydrated.

2 Dig a hole and make a mound in the middle for the roots to sit over. You can usually see a dark area on the trunk of the plant where the soil initially came up to. Make sure the hole is deep enough so this dark line is at finished ground level, and below the graft point if the plant is grafted.

3 Place the plant in the hole and spread the roots over the mound.

4 Mix compost or manure into the extracted soil, and then put the soil back in the hole. Push soil under and around all the roots. Water and apply mulch.

planting hole should be about twice as deep as the width of the bulb. This means small bulbs are planted near the soil surface while larger bulbs are planted much more deeply. There are some exceptions to these rules. Many extremely large bulbs, such as those of crinum, lilium and belladonna lilies, are planted on or at the soil surface.

For all bulbs, select a situation that's well drained and where the bulbs can easily emerge from the soil and grow into the sun.

Bare-rooted specimens

Bare-rooted plants that are grown in production nurseries are dug up to be sold when they are dormant. Most have soil removed from their roots but some are transported with their root systems still in soil and wrapped in hessian or plastic. Where the soil has been removed, the root system is protected from drying out or damage with a temporary sleeve of plastic, packed with coir peat or sphagnum moss.

Bare-rooted plants should be returned to the soil (or transferred to a pot with potting mix) before they begin to regrow. Remove all soil and packaging material before replanting. This is important whether the plant is going into soil or a pot. To remove the soil, shake the plant gently.

It may be necessary to trim damaged roots before the plant goes back into the soil. For more details on planting bare-rooted specimens, see Step-by-Step, left.

Planting seedlings

Seedlings are small plants, usually vegetables or flowering annuals, raised from seed and sold in punnets or small cells. They are cheap to buy or can be raised at home by sowing seed (see Chapter 3 for more information about growing from seed). Seedlings are relatively inexpensive to buy. Flowering annuals bought as seedlings can be used as accent plants to add a bold dash of colour to your garden, as mass planting to cover large areas, or to dress up a container.

Careful removal of the seedling from its punnet or cell and planting with correct spacing between plants are the two fundamentals to getting seedlings off to a good start in their new spot.

Once they are growing, they need regular water, liquid feeding and protection from pests including slugs, snails, caterpillars and aphids. Use organic insecticides to protect plants.

Step-by-Step

DIVIDING AND PLANTING SEEDLINGS

1 Many seedlings come in punnets that hold about six or eight plants. To remove the seedling from a cell, pinch the bottom of the punnet and the seedling should pop straight out. Start dividing the seedlings by splitting the rootball in half.

2 If the seedlings are together in one punnet, gently pull the roots apart. Aim to have one or two seedlings in each division. If the roots are difficult to separate, try soaking the plants.

3 Use a trowel to dig a small hole about twice the width of the rootball of the seedling. Place the seedling into the hole. Follow the recommended spacing of the seedlings as shown on the label, and continue planting.

4 Mulch around the plants with organic mulch such as sugar cane or lucerne. Water well.

OPPOSITE Annuals including vegetables are sold as seedlings. These are bought in punnets or cells.
ABOVE LEFT Mulch around the plants when the seedling is planted.

How to plant grafted plants

A grafted plant is one that is joined to another to combine the desirable attributes of the two plants, and can be used, for example, to create disease-resistant rootstock. The point on the plant where the two meet is known as the graft union. It is usually noticeable on a plant as the bark may vary in colour or the stem may vary in diameter at the point of union. Leafy growth and branching occurs above the graft union, with roots forming below the graft.

The plant material below the graft union is known as the rootstock, and above the graft union is the scion. Plants are generally grafted low on the stem, however grafted standard plants may have a graft union that's up to 1 m above the base of the plant.

When planting a grafted plant, locate the graft union and ensure it is at or above soil level.

Regularly check the graft union for signs of damage and insect pests, and for any shoots from below the graft—these should be removed from

ABOVE Many ornamental blossom trees are grown from grafted plants.

the rootstock below the graft, cut off flush with the stem or roots or ripped off. Deter further shoots from growing below the graft union by regularly rubbing off any new growth that appears while it is still young and soft.

If shoots from the rootstock area are allowed to grow there is a high risk that the plant will lose its vigour, as the energy is directed into the new growth rather than the main plant.

Nitrogen drawdown

A funny thing can happen when you put woody mulch on top of soil. Your plants' health can actually go backwards, despite all the benefits mulch provides such as insulating roots, conserving moisture and stopping weed growth. The first indication that something's amiss is yellowing foliage. This poor growth is due to nitrogen drawdown. As the mulch lies on the soil surface, it begins to break down. This decomposition process is undertaken by micro-organisms, fungi and bacteria in the soil that need nitrogen to fuel their growth.

To overcome nitrogen drawdown, use a 2 cm layer of compost or aged manure or a sprinkle of blood and bone or other fertiliser beneath coarse, woody mulch to provide the extra nitrogen the micro-organisms use in decomposition.

Using mulch

The job isn't finished when the plant goes into the ground—you will also need to apply mulch.

How to apply

Mulch is widely used to help plants grow and should be applied around all new plantings. The current trend is not to apply mulch too thickly as a dense layer of mulch can stop rain and irrigation from reaching the roots. It has also been shown that soil under very heavy layers of coarse mulch can become water repellent. Mulches should not be piled up around the stem or trunk, as this can lead to collar rot or fungal problems in the root system, which lead to dieback or death.

For best results, use a thin layer of fine mulch, such as compost, topped with a layer of coarse organic mulch. The combined depth of both fine and coarse mulch can vary from 2–5 cm, depending on the mulches used.

Commercially available organic mulches include a variety of composts, such as sugar cane, chopped lucerne, bark fines, rice hulls, woodchip and tea tree but there are many other mulches and all work well. It's a good idea to choose a mulch that can easily break down to enrich the soil, is locally available, and that's easy to apply as this will be both the cheapest and most environmentally sustainable selection.

See Chapter 9 for more tips on how to care for your plant once it is in the ground.

TOP Use organic mulches to protect plant roots and nourish soils.
CENTRE Apply mulch loosely but not too thickly around new planting. A depth of 2.5 cm is sufficient.
LEFT When planting, be sure to fill the area around the rootball with soil or organic garden mix to completely cover the root system.

CHAPTER 3

Growing from seed

Why do I need to read this chapter?

- ✿ To find out how to grow plants from seed.
- ✿ To discover the tricks of breaking seed dormancy.
- ✿ To find out how to collect, prepare and store seed.

The birds and the bees

There are two main sources of new plants. The first is seed, and the second is newly rooted material grown from an established plant. This second method is called vegetative propagation and is discussed in the next chapter.

Seed-grown plants range from being very similar to the parent that produced the seed, to differing wildly, much as children differ from their parents and from their siblings.

To control the appearance of a seed-grown plant, the seed grower must control the source of pollen (the male contribution to the seed) and select the ovary (the female part of the equation), which receives the pollen. If a seed-grown plant resembles its parent it is said to come 'true'. Some plants can be relied on to come true even where there's no control over the pollination process. These plants are often referred to as open-pollinated plants. Many vegetable seeds grown in gardens that are referred to as heirloom seed varieties are open pollinated. Some heirloom seeds that are prized for their flavour or growth are so treasured they have been passed on from generation to generation within a family. A gardener may be growing the same variety as their grandparents, or perhaps even earlier generations, grew and enjoyed.

Seeds that have been crossed to provide a plant with specific characteristics, such as large fruit, are described as hybrids or cultivars. The hybrid progeny may have been bred by selectively crossing plants over several generations. They do not normally come 'true' through open pollination. These hybrid plants must be regrown from seed that has been formed by recrossing, using the same parents or by growing from cuttings or some other means of vegetative propagation.

ABOVE Bees foraging among flowers for food carry pollen from one plant to another and so help to fertilise flowers for seed production.
OPPOSITE Grow flowers among crops to attract helpful pollinators.

The importance of bees

Bees are vital to the production of fruit and seeds because they transfer pollen from one plant to another as they forage for food. While some plants are self-pollinated, most rely on bees, small insects or animals to transfer their pollen from one plant to another. Some plants rely on the wind to disperse their pollen.

There are many varieties of bees but the European honeybee is found across the world and is the major pollinating insect. Deaths in bee colonies and the reduction in bee numbers in some parts of the world due to pests, diseases, pesticide use, starvation and habitat loss threaten food production on a global scale.

To do your part to create a bee-friendly environment, add bee-attracting plants, such as daisies, lavender, borage, crimson clover, buckwheat, foxgloves, thyme, coriander, rosemary, summer savory and bee balm, to your garden, and use as little pesticide as possible. Bees are primarily attracted by certain colours, particularly blue, and by markings that direct the insect to the centre of the flower. Blue flowers often have very little scent because the colour is sufficient to attract bees.

There are more than 1500 species of Australian native bees and these insects are excellent pollinators that can be safely introduced to vegetable gardens and orchards to ensure good crop pollination. While they produce little in the way of honey compared with honeybees, they do a good job in spreading pollen between plants. Native bees are generally stingless and are active when temperatures rise above 18°C. Native bees and hives can be bought commercially.

How to grow plants from seed

One of the cheapest and easiest ways to grow a new plant is to grow it from seed. You can purchase seed at nurseries and other retail outlets, or from mail-order suppliers. You can also produce your own seed once your plants produce flowers and their fruit matures.

As well as being easy and cheap to obtain, seed allows you greater control over quantity than you would get with seedlings. By sowing a few seeds of a productive plant every few weeks, you stagger the maturity of your crop so you are harvesting over a longer period and avoid a glut where all your crop matures simultaneously.

Seed sowing methods

Seeds can be sown directly into the garden in the position in which they are to grow. This is termed direct sowing.

If you are just starting out with growing from seed, begin with a seed that's easy to handle and that germinates readily and quickly, such as peas or beans (see the lists of easy-to-grow seeds for vegetable and flower gardens on page 39).

However, most seeds are best started off in a container rather than planted directly into the soil. This is because it is easier to control the growing environment in a container. If you are impatient and just want to scatter seeds into the garden or plant them straight into the vegie patch, stick to large seeds such as peas, sweet peas, sunflowers and broad beans.

Seeds can be sown into small containers such as punnets, seed trays (also referred to as flats) or other pots, so they grow to seedling stage before being transplanted into the garden.

It is best to use shallow containers, so grow seeds in punnets, seed trays, small pots or even egg cartons. Whatever you use, make sure the container has drainage holes in its base. If you are using a pot made from biodegradable material such as coir peat or cardboard, it is possible to transplant the seedling into the garden without removing it from its container.

Reused punnets or pots must be clean and sterile. Hose or rinse them thoroughly in disinfectant, such as diluted Dettol, bleach or tea-tree oil.

To avoid disease, use purchased seed-raising mix, which is sterile. Hose or rinse them off, then wash them thoroughly. Other products that can be used include vermiculite, perlite or a homemade mix of coir

Step-by-Step

HOW TO MAKE A NEWSPAPER POT

1 Fold a sheet of newspaper in half, and then fold in half again lengthways until it's about 20 cm wide.

2 Place a tall straight-sided glass, about 15 cm high, at one end of the newspaper. The open end of the glass should have about a quarter of the width of the newspaper beyond it. Roll the paper around the glass.

3 Stand the glass up and push the newspaper into the open end of the glass. This becomes the base of the pot.

4 Pull out the glass and stand the newspaper pot on its base. Push the bottom of the glass back into the pot to flatten and firm the newspaper base.

peat and propagating sand. Don't use garden soil in seed-raising punnets or other containers.

As a rule of thumb, larger seeds are planted a little more deeply than small, fine seeds. The seed packet will give all the information you need about planting depth, sowing times and the expected length of time between sowing and seeing the first tiny shoots appear.

After planting, maintain the seed-raising mix so it is moist but not too wet. Keep seed trays warm while you are waiting for germination by popping them into a homemade glasshouse, such as a foam box with a piece of glass over it. Keep it out of direct sunlight.

Thinning out

If you've sown seeds thickly and they all shoot, gently thin them out leaving only the strongest seedlings. This step is called 'thinning out' and is also done if seeds are direct sown into the soil. Do this while the seedlings are still quite small (around 12 mm high). This step may seem a waste, but overcrowding leads to fungal diseases such as damping off. You may lose your entire crop if you let all the seedlings grow.

Once they are large enough to handle (usually when they've formed two true leaves), either plant them out into well-prepared soil in the garden, or pot them on into a slightly larger container with potting mix.

Step-by-Step

HOW TO SOW SEEDS INTO TRAYS

1 Half fill a seed tray or small pot with propagating mix.

2 Place one or two seeds into each cell of the seed tray.

3 Lightly cover seeds with propagating mix.

4 Water. Cover with a plastic bag or lid.

ABOVE Save money and recycle by sowing seeds into homemade newspaper tubes or recycled toilet paper rolls.

Easy-to-grow edibles from seed

As a rule of thumb, large seeds are easier to grow than small seeds. However, size alone does not determine ease of growing. Seeds that sprout readily are generally less prone to disease and less sensitive to temperature and other climatic triggers. As many seeds only germinate at certain soil temperatures, sowing at the right time of the year is an important key to successful seed raising.

Plant	Best season to sow
Beans	Spring to early autumn
Beetroot	Late winter to early autumn; spring to summer only in cold zones
Broad beans	Early autumn to late winter
Carrot	Year round but late winter to late summer best
Cucumber	Spring to autumn
Parsley	All year but late winter to late summer best
Peas	Autumn to spring
Pumpkin	Spring to summer
Rocket	Year round
Sweet corn	Spring to autumn
Tomato	Late winter to autumn; year round in warm climates
Watermelon	Late spring to summer

Easy-to-grow flowers from seed

As with vegetable seeds, size alone isn't a guide to ease of propagation. It is important to sow in the right season.

Flower	Best season to sow
Alyssum	Late winter to autumn
Aquilegia	Late summer to autumn
Calendula	Summer to autumn
Californian poppy	Late winter to summer
Candytuft	Summer to autumn
Cleome	Late winter to autumn
Honesty	Summer to autumn
Marigold	Spring to summer
Mexican sunflower	Spring to summer; year round in warm climates
Sunflower	Late spring to summer
Sweet pea	Autumn to spring
Virginia stock	Autumn

RIGHT Cleome grows easily from seed and will self sow in gardens. It has many small seeds in long seed pods.
OPPOSITE Peas are best planted between autumn and spring and will generally be ready for harvest 10–12 weeks after planting.

Exposure to smoke

Enzymes in bushfire smoke may trigger germination in dormant seeds in fire-prone areas, allowing them to recolonise an area after a fire. Rather than set fire to your seeds, you can apply the enzymes another way. Smoke-infused water (sold as smoke water) is available commercially. Soak your seeds in the water to reproduce the reaction your seed would have to bushfire. Alternatively, place the seeds in a container near a smoky fire made from gum leaves. The germination of Australian native plants including *Verticordia, Conospermum, Eriostemon, Hybanthus, Leschenaultia, Pimelea, Stirlingia, Geleznowia, Calytrix, Actinotus* and members of the Epacridaceae family along with some South African native plants is triggered by this method.

Understanding seed dormancy

Seeds have evolved mechanisms to allow them to germinate when they have the best chance of growth and survival. This may mean that a seed can lie dormant in soil for months or even years until the right conditions exist for its growth.

Seeds with inbuilt dormancy may be stored for long periods or can exist in the soil for extremely long periods. One of the oldest seeds ever to germinate was a date seed, estimated by carbon dating to be 2000 years old. The seed, which was discovered in the 1960s, is thought to have survived for two millennia preserved by the hot, dry climate and arid conditions of the Dead Sea in Israel. This is quite a rare

case—for most plants, heat damages the seed's embryo.

Seed dormancy is broken either by physical or chemical conditions. By imitating these conditions, it is possible to artificially break the period of dormancy and allow germination. Factors that can break the dormancy of seed include exposure to low temperatures, light or the lack thereof, moisture, damage to the seed coat, partial digestion by animals, treating with gibberellic acid (a plant hormone), or even exposure to smoke.

Some plants require special conditions even after germination for successful growth. For example, some seeds must be grown in the presence of other organisms, such as fungi, to allow them to succeed.

While some seeds may be dormant for extended periods of time, others have no period of dormancy. If they are not provided with suitable growing conditions immediately after they are released by their parent plant, they may fail to grow. This ability for a seed to germinate is referred to as its viability. Seeds may have low viability or lose viability over time.

Plants that lack inbuilt dormancy and that have low viability need to be sown quickly after harvest. Failure of some seed to germinate after planting may be the result of the age of the seed and poor viability. Parsnip seed is one commonly grown seed that quickly loses viability.

RIGHT Soak peas and sweet peas overnight in water then plant immediately. The moisture stimulates germination.

OPPOSITE Pimelea is an Australian native shrub that germinates more reliably when grown from seed exposed to smoked water.

Protecting seeds and seedlings

Seeds and small seedlings are highly vulnerable to damage from birds. Birds such as blackbirds and pigeons, along with many native birds, are quite partial to newly emerged or newly planted seedlings and may also remove seed from the soil before germination.

One way to protect a large planting of seedlings is to place a long, low tunnel over the crop. Such a tunnel is easily and cheaply constructed from wire hoops, pipe such as 13 mm polythene irrigation pipe, or wire and bird-safe mesh.

If using wire, cut 2 or 3 gauge wire into 60 cm lengths and bend them over the new plantings to form hoops. Push the hoops firmly into the soil, spacing them about 40 cm apart, along your row of seedlings. Once the framework is in place, stretch netting or wire mesh over the hoops and secure it at both ends and along each side. Use tent pegs or pieces of wire to secure the netting to the ground. Select double woven nylon net or lightweight shadecloth.

Fertilise your plants and water them well before you cover them. To provide ongoing water, either lift up part of the mesh to provide the room for your hose or sprinkler or, better still, run a dripline along the seedling row to take the pain out of watering.

As well as stopping the birds getting access, the tunnel protects the seedlings from any late frost, cold winds or from that neighbourhood cat that wants to dig in your garden bed. When your plants are no longer vulnerable, remove the tunnel and erect it over your next batch of fledgling seedlings.

Step-by-Step

HOW TO MAKE A SEEDLING TUNNEL

1 Plant the seedlings, fertilise, mulch and water well. To make the hoops, cut 13 mm irrigation pipe or wire into 60 cm lengths.

2 Push the hoops firmly into the soil. Space them about 40 cm apart.

3 Stretch shadecloth or netting over the hoops.

4 Secure at each end and along the sides with tent pegs.

OPPOSITE A glass cloche can be used to protect seedlings from frost or pests. Remove it on hot or sunny days.

Saving seeds

It is the very nature of gardening and gardeners to nurture, recycle and reuse, and the treatment of seeds is no exception. If you've harvested a particularly tasty or easy-to-grow vegie from your backyard plot, you'll be keen to grow that plant again so you can enjoy the flavour another time. The easiest way to do this is to collect some of its seeds.

If the seeds you want to save come from an open-pollinated vegetable variety, rather than a hybrid, then those seeds should grow into a plant that has the same characteristics as the parent. This feature is known as coming true to type. Most heritage or heirloom varieties come true to type and are the best varieties to grow if you want

to save seed to resow in your garden. Seeds from hybrids, particularly those plants sold as F1 Hybrids, do not always come true to the parent plant, but reflect the 'grandparents' or a previous generation that was crossed to produce the plant. This means the crop grown from saved seed may be inferior to the one you grew originally. For this reason it is not usually worthwhile to save seeds from F1 Hybrids.

As well as providing more of the plants you want to grow, seed saving is economical. Once you start saving seed, you don't have to outlay more money on seeds—unless, of course, you want to buy a new variety. You can also swap your seeds with those saved by other gardeners. But it is not only an economical habit to get into. Saving

ABOVE LEFT If you have a variety that will come true from seed, leave a portion of each crop to mature, before harvesting the seed.
ABOVE RIGHT Even crops normally grown for leaf, such as rocket and cabbage, flower and seed if left to mature.

seed from your best crops allows you to keep growing plants that you know will do well in your climate and soil. By continuing to grow varieties that prosper, have good yields and taste good, gardeners preserve their heritage in their garden.

Tip To remind yourself when it is time to replant, store your seeds in a box divided into months or seasons.

Keeping seed

Some seed must be replanted immediately, but other seed needs to be kept until the best growing season returns. Store your seed for replanting so that it stays as fresh as possible for optimum rates of germination. You will need to keep seed clean and free of pests or disease. Keep seed fresh by storing it in an airtight container, or wrapped in foil, in a cool, dark place. Make sure it is clearly labelled with its name, including the variety if you know it.

ABOVE LEFT Have a secure spot to store unused and saved seed.
ABOVE RIGHT To harvest seeds from a tomato for replanting, allow some fruit to remain on the plant at the end of the season. Pick when fully ripe.

Seed saving tips

The following tips will increase your success rate when saving seeds.

- For leafy plants, such as rocket and silverbeet, leave plants to mature so they flower and set seed.
- For fruiting plants where the seed is contained inside the fruit, such as tomatoes and pumpkins, allow the fruit to thoroughly ripen before removing the seeds.
- Remove seed from pulp, clean it, then allow the seeds to dry.
- Select seeds from the healthiest plants that had the best flowers or fruit, or that coped well with seasonal extremes and were not susceptible to pests or diseases.
- Store seed in an airtight container in a cool, dark spot.
- Always label seed with its name and date of harvest.

Also include the date you collected the seed, so you know it's fresh when the time comes to replant your seed.

To help create a repository for old, unused and heirloom varieties, some keen gardeners established a group called Seed Savers Network. Members grow and harvest heirloom crops, saving a portion of each crop's seed to be shared by other gardeners in the network. Seed Savers Network is now active in many parts of Australia. Visit www.seedsavers.net for more information on where to join.

CHAPTER 4

Plant propagation

Why do I need to read this chapter?

- To discover the art of propagating plants from cuttings.

- To learn how to grow new plants by division, grafting and layering.

- To understand other methods of plant propagation.

Alternative methods of planting

Growing plants from seed is discussed in Chapter 3—but there are other ways to propagate plants so the new plant is identical, or 'true', to its parent. These methods are forms of asexual propagation or cloning. It may sound like the stuff of science fiction but in reality it is using the natural properties of the plant to reproduce more plants.

In the wild, some plants are capable of regenerating from a stem that's broken off, by suckering from their root system, or from branches that lie on the ground, forming roots. By using the same principles, it is possible to grow a new plant from a small part taken from the stem or root system of an existing plant.

If you are just starting to experiment with propagating your own plants, begin with easy-to-grow plants to master a basic understanding of what's involved (see 'Easy growing', page 53).

Cuttings are the most widely used form of asexual plant propagation. A cutting is the name given to a piece of plant, usually the stem, but sometimes the roots or leaves, which can be used to grow a new plant. Cuttings are also referred to as slips.

Many plants, particularly shrubs and perennials, can be grown from cuttings. A cutting-grown plant is identical to the parent plant and a useful way to

propagate a cultivated variety (also called a cultivar) that may not come true from seed.

Cuttings can be taken at different times of the year and from different parts of the plant, but for most plants, there is an optimum type of cutting and time of the year for propagation. For the range of cuttings see 'Types of cuttings', above.

Some cuttings readily form roots, while others require the addition of plant growth hormones, special propagating medium and controlled temperature and moisture levels. Plants can take from a few days to more than a year to form roots; however, most cuttings start to form roots within two to three weeks of propagation. When cuttings form roots, they are said 'to strike' or 'have struck'.

Types of cuttings

Different types of cuttings that are used in plant propagation relate to the stage of growth of the parent plant, the season and the part of the plant that's used. Plant stems are most widely used. Here's a quick guide to types of stem cutting and time of year to take them for the best results.

Cutting material	Other names	Season
Soft tip	Softwood	Spring (or when new growth available)
Semi-hardwood	Half ripe	Late spring to autumn
Hardwood	Ripe	Late summer–early winter (evergreen); autumn to winter (deciduous)
Herbaceous		Any time
Heel		Any time

ABOVE Salvias grow readily from cuttings and make a good plant for beginners.

Types of cuttings

The three main types of cuttings are soft tip, semi-hardwood and hardwood, and each of these have special requirements for growing success.

Soft tip cuttings

Soft tip cuttings are taken from new growth while it is still soft. They consist of a growing tip and small length of stem with several nodes (the point at which the shoots are forming). Soft tip cuttings are usually 5–12 cm long but can be as small as 2–4 cm. To minimise wilting, take a longer piece than is needed and cut it to size while preparing your cutting.

As the plant is actively growing, soft tip cuttings are usually quick to strike (often within seven to 10 days of taking the cutting). They are also prone to wilting, so keep the cutting well hydrated when collected and once potted up.

Store cuttings in water until they are ready for planting. Once planted, soft tip cuttings should be misted regularly and protected from drying out under a glass or plastic cover. This can be in a glasshouse or cold frame, in a propagating unit or by covering the pot of cuttings with a plastic bag.

To prepare a soft tip cutting for planting, trim the base of each of the cuttings to just below a node so each includes a tip and several nodes. Remove the lower leaves, dip the base of the cutting in hormone

Step-by-Step

HOW TO TAKE SOFT TIP CUTTINGS

1   Take a 5–12 cm cutting of the soft new growth. It should have several nodes.

2   Remove the lower leaves.

3   Trim the base of the cutting to just below a node.

4   Fill a small pot with propagating mix and make several holes around the edge with a pencil or dibbler.

5   Dip the base of the cutting in rooting hormone powder or gel.

6   Insert the cutting into the pot. You should be able to fit about five or six into a 10 cm diameter pot.

7   Make two hoops with wire—cut-up wire coat hangers are good to use—and insert to make a frame over the cuttings. Cover with a plastic bag and secure it around the pot with an elastic band to create a mini hothouse.

rooting powder and insert at least half the length of the stem into coarse propagating medium or well-drained potting mix.

Many cuttings, particularly soft tip cuttings, form roots more quickly when there is a difference in temperature between the top and bottom of the cutting. This is achieved by providing bottom heat via a heat mat or heating unit and misting top growth.

After placing cuttings into pots or trays, always mark them clearly with a label to identify the name of the plant and the date you took the cutting.

Semi-hardwood cuttings

These cuttings are easier to manage than soft tip cuttings but can be slower to strike. They are taken after the new growth has firmed but is still flexible. Identify the cutting material by its colour as the stem changes colour from green to brown as it matures. It is best to take semi-hardwood cuttings in late spring or summer, but it's still possible to take them in early autumn after summer growth has matured.

Semi-hardwood cuttings are generally 8–15 cm long, and include several nodes. If the cutting has a soft tip, remove it as it may wilt. Also remove leaves on the lower half or two-thirds of the cutting. Cut large leaves in half to reduce moisture loss and allow more cuttings to be placed into a pot or tray.

Semi-hardwood cuttings strike well in pots filled with propagating mix

Step-by-Step

HOW TO TAKE SEMI-HARDWOOD CUTTINGS

1 Take 8–15 cm long cuttings that include several nodes.

2 Remove the soft tip and any flowers and buds.

3 Strip or prune off the leaves on the lower half or two-thirds of the cutting.

4 Dip the base of the cutting in rooting hormone, then insert into a pot filled with propagating mix. Keep cuttings in a brightly lit spot out of direct sun.

with several cuttings in each pot. Before inserting into the coarse propagating mix, dip the end in a rooting hormone to maximise the strike rate.

Semi-hardwood cuttings need to be kept kept well-watered and misted until such time as the roots form. However, they are not as prone to

Step-by-Step

HOW TO TRAIN A STANDARD FUCHSIA

1 Choose a strong, upright plant with well-established roots.

2 Transfer the plant to a larger pot and attach the stem to a bamboo stick.

3 As the plant grows, continue to tie it to the supporting stake.

4 When the plant reaches the desired height, pinch prune the growing tip to encourage branches.

5 Remove all lower growth.

Tip Cuttings strike best when grown in a well-drained medium. You can buy ready-made propagating mixes by the bag from your local nursery or you can make your own by combining equal amounts of sharp or propagating sand (a coarse, washed river sand) and coir peat. Perlite can be substituted for sand.

ABOVE These hardwood cuttings have been prepared for planting.

ABOVE Cut large leaves in half to reduce moisture loss before roots form.

wilting as soft tip cuttings. To maintain extra humidity around cuttings, cover with a plastic bag or cloche.

Hardwood cuttings

These may be taken from evergreen or deciduous plants. They are best taken late in the growing season or, in the case of deciduous plants, after leaf drop while the plant is dormant. These cuttings are generally pencil thick (thicker than semi-hardwood cuttings) and long enough to include several nodes. These cuttings are usually around 15–30 cm in length.

Evergreen hardwood cuttings are generally placed in a pot with coarse sand or free-draining potting mix without a covering, but deciduous hardwood cuttings can be planted in the open ground. Expect roots to form in spring. Rooting hormone specifically formulated for hardwood cuttings increases strike rates.

Step-by-Step

HOW TO TAKE HARDWOOD CUTTINGS

1 Take cuttings about 15–30 cm long. They should be close to the thickness of a pencil. Remove the tip of the cuttings.

2 Remove the leaves (if any) on the lower half or two-thirds of the cutting.

3 Dip the base of the cutting in rooting hormone powder or gel, then insert cuttings into a pot filled with propagating mix.

Hints when collecting cuttings

The following are some tips that will help optimise your strike rates when you take a cutting.

1 **Health of mother plant**

   Success with striking cuttings can relate back to the health of the plant from which the cutting was taken. The parent plant is referred to as the mother plant. A young, vigorously growing mother plant will provide healthy cuttings that are more likely to grow. Ensure the plant that you are getting your cutting from is well prepared, and water it well so it is not wilting.

2 **How many cuttings?**

   Take cuttings from all over the plant. Always take several cuttings even if you only want to grow one plant, as strike rates vary.

3 **Keep them cool**

   To keep the cuttings in good condition until they can be planted, wrap them in moist newspaper or a tea towel, put them in an plastic bag and store them in a Esky with a cold brick.

4 **Timing**

   The best time to take cuttings is early in the morning.

5 **Flowers and fruit**

   Before you plant your cuttings, ensure you remove all the flowers and fruit.

6 **Right way up**

   If a cutting has no leaves or growing shoot, it can be tricky to distinguish top and bottom once the cutting is removed from the mother plant. It is vital to plant a cutting the correct way up or it can't form roots. To mark top from bottom make a straight cut across the bottom of the cutting and a slanting cut across the top. As a general guide, buds point upwards.

RIGHT After taking cuttings, always mark them clearly with a label to identify the name of the plant and the date you took the cutting.

Easy growing

Here are some plants that are generally easy to grow from stem cuttings. Start with these and when you master the art of growing from cuttings move on to plants that are more challenging. As well as the plants listed below, most succulent-stemmed plants or plants with lots of nodes along a stem are generally easier to grow from cuttings.

Name	Cutting method	Season
Agave attenuata	Hardwood	Year round
Box	Soft tip	Spring to summer
Box	Semi-hardwood	Late spring to autumn
Coleus	Semi-hardwood	Late spring to autumn
Crassula	Hardwood	Year round
Daisy (eg Marguerite)	Semi-hardwood	Spring to autumn
Frangipani	Hardwood	Autumn to winter
Geranium (eg zonal, ivy, regal pelargonium)	Semi-hardwood	Spring to autumn
Hydrangea	Hardwood	Autumn to winter
Impatiens	Semi-hardwood	Spring to autumn
Lavender	Soft tip	Spring
Plectranthus	Semi-hardwood	Late spring to autumn
Rosemary	Soft tip	Spring
Rosemary	Semi-hardwood	Late spring to autumn
Salvia	Semi-hardwood	Late spring to autumn

Growing by division

As well as taking a piece of stem to grow a new plant you can actually divide one plant to form several new plants, each with its own leaves, stem and root system. This process is called division and is used to propagate plants that form a clump including shrubs, perennials, bulbs and grasses.

Some plants naturally form offshoots, also known as pups. These can be detached or divided from the parent plant, and once planted will go on to form their own root system. Pups are found around the base of many bromeliads and succulents. They are detached when they are large enough to handle and can be treated like cuttings or, if they have already developed their own root system, potted up or planted directly in the garden.

Dividing perennials

There are two groups of perennial plants. Herbaceous perennials, such as salvia, chrysanthemum and achillea, that die down over winter. Evergreen perennials, such as agapanthus and clivia, don't die back, but remain leafy.

Perennials are the horticultural equivalent of Norman Lindsay's Magic Pudding. You can even dig up a perennial, chop it up, replant it and it still keeps on growing.

Lifting and dividing perennials provides new plants for free, but is also a way to revitalise old plants for

Step-by-Step

HOW TO DIVIDE PERENNIALS

1 Before digging up a dormant, herbaceous perennial, cut back any dead growth. Use a fork or spade to dig up the perennial plant so you can lift the roots clear of the soil.

2 Shake the clump free of loose dirt and remove weeds and dead leaves.

3 Use a spade, trowel, or knife to divide the clump into several sections each with some roots and a crown (and leaves if it is an evergreen perennial such as agapanthus). Remove any unhealthy or diseased parts.

4 Use secateurs to tidy up any damaged or broken pieces. Remove large leaves from evergreen perennials to reduce water loss.

5 Replant part of the clump into the original spot then use the divided pieces elsewhere in the garden, give them to friends or pot them up.

Plants to divide in winter or early spring

Virtually any clumping plant can be divided to provide lots of new plants for your garden. Dividing also reinvigorates a clump. Winter or very early spring are generally the best times to divide most garden plants, before they come into active growth. Also take the opportunity to renourish soil before replanting.

Plants suitable for dividing this way include: acanthus, achillea, agapanthus, ajuga, artemisia, aster, bamboo, campanula (herbaceous), canna, ceratostigma, chrysanthemum, clivia, dicentra, dietes, echinacea, erigeron, festuca, geranium (*Geranium* spp.), gerbera, geum, ginger, helenium, Japanese windflower (*Anemone* x *hybrida*, *A. hupehensis*), kangaroo paw (*Anigozanthos* spp.), kniphofia, lambs' ear (*Stachys byzantina*), liriope, may (*Spiraea* spp.), mondo grass, ornamental grasses, penstemon, phlox, physostegia, rhubarb, rudbeckia, salvia, shasta daisy (*Leucanthemum* x *superbum*), solidago, stokes aster, thalictrum, thyme, tree dahlia, water lily.

ABOVE Clumping perennials like these agapanthus can be divided into several new plants—a great way to create a border planting.

improved flowering and growth. If a perennial plant hasn't been flowering well or has dead patches, it will benefit from being divided.

To revitalise your clump, divide perennials every three years. The extra plants you gain while doing this task are a bonus to be used elsewhere in the garden, or give away to friends or neighbours, or the local fete.

How to divide a clump

This technique works for any clumping plant you wish to divide. You need a garden fork, a sharp spade and a pair of sharp secateurs to get started. You can lift (that is dig up) and divide (that is chop up) most herbaceous and evergreen perennials any time from late winter until early spring before plants resume active growth.

If the herbaceous perennial clump has died off but not yet been cut back, cut it back to ground level before you begin digging. If it is green and leafy just start digging (see page 54, opposite, for a step-by-step approach).

Established plants are usually divided into about three new plants, but how many new plants you get is dependent upon how many you want, and the size of your parent plant. Remember, each division must have some roots, some stem (called a crown) and, if it's evergreen, some leaves.

To get the best from your plant after it has been divided, revitalise the soil it has been growing in by digging in compost or aged manure and an all-purpose fertiliser such as blood and bone. If your soil is prone to drying out, also dig in water-holding crystals (polymer-based granules that store moisture in soils and potting mix). When using these products, always follow the instructions on the container

carefully so you don't use too many—an excess will swell up, pushing the plants out of the soil. The final step is to water the freshly dug soil well, then it's ready to be replanted.

As you return the divided perennial to its garden bed, take care not to replant it too deeply. It is important to keep the crown level with the top of the soil. Remember, this plant will grow up and out in all directions, so allow space for regrowth.

Water evergreen perennials well after dividing and give them a dose of liquid seaweed extract to encourage strong root growth. As herbaceous perennials begin to reshoot, be sure to increase their water. Stand back and watch the growth and expansion begin.

Step-by-Step

REPOTTING A CYMBIDIUM ORCHID

1 Cymbidium orchids flower best when their roots fill the pot, but when they start to look straggly or stop flowering it's time to repot them. The ideal timing is every two or three years in spring, after flowering. Pull the orchid out of the old pot. Sometimes they slide out easily but you may need to break the pot to get them out.

2 Start pulling off the dead and old, shrivelled bulbs. Split up the orchid by using an old knife or a pruning saw, or pulling it apart.

3 Split the orchid into sections so that each has leaves, a new shoot and three or four firm bulbs. These are the bulbs without leaves, which continue to provide the flowering stems with nutrients.

4 Place several sections around the edge of the new pot. Backfill with orchid potting mix. Add a handful of slow-release fertiliser for orchids to each pot and water well.

Tip Cymbidium orchids are usually grown in pots with bark-based orchid potting mix, but can also be grown outdoors in warm areas by creating a planting zones filled with orchid potting mix. They grow well under trees.

How to divide an orchid

Regular division of the clump is also important for cymbidium orchids. For an indication of how often to do this task, be guided by the size of the plant. Orchids that have filled their pots with growth flower better if they are divided in early spring. Plant each new division in a pot that is large enough to allow at least two years of growth. Use fresh potting mix for orchids (a free-draining, coarse, bark-based mix available at nurseries or hardware stores or made up with a 50:50 blend of orchid bark and coir peat).

Place the pots in a sheltered spot where they receive bright light. Keep orchids outside in a brightly lit position for good growth before moving them into full view when the flower spikes start to form in late autumn and early winter. Protect plants from cold conditions in frosty areas. Feed plants again in late summer when blooms are initiated for winter flowering.

OPPOSITE Cymbidiums flower winter to spring.

Layering

Many ground cover plants reproduce themselves through a process of natural layering. As they spread across the ground, roots form from their nodes. These layered branches are called runners. Once a plant has formed roots from its runners these pieces can be detached and replanted. Plants that naturally grow by forming runners include strawberry, jasmine, kikuyu and couch grasses, and ivy.

Even plants that don't naturally form runners can be propagated by layering. This is because branches from some plants form roots if they are brought in contact with the soil.

There are two layering methods used for home garden propagation: ground or simple layering and aerial layering. Layering is often used for plants that are difficult to grow from cuttings.

Simple layering

To grow a new plant by this method of layering, select a strong-growing, flexible side branch near the base of the plant. Bend it to the ground so that a node (the point at which the shoots are forming) touches the soil. Remove any side branches but leave the tip. The underside of the branch around the node can be gently nicked or scraped to remove a small piece of the outer bark to reveal the area below, known as the cambium layer. To do this, use a sharp knife such as a budding or grafting knife or a blade of your

Step-by-Step

HOW TO PROPAGATE BY LAYERING

1   Choose a long flexible stem.

2   Make a 45° slice about a third of the way through the stem with a sharp knife, such as a budding knife, on the side that will be in contact with the soil.

3   Pin the part of the stem that has been sliced to the ground with a wire peg.

4   Stake the end of the stem so it's upright. When roots have formed at the cut point and the stem has started to grow new leaves, the stem from the parent plant can be severed and the new plant dug up and replanted.

LEFT AND ABOVE Both climbing roses (left) and daphne (above) lend themselves well to simple layering techniques.

secateurs. It is from this point roots grow. Cover over the stem with soil but allow the shoot to protrude out. Hold the layered branch in place with a piece of bent wire or some flat stones. Expect the branch to take around three months to form a viable root system. Separate and plant.

Simple layering can be used to successfully propagate azalea, rhododendron, daphne, box, camellia, climbing roses, honeysuckle and forsythia, as well as Australian natives such as boronia and westringia.

If the branch is long enough, it can be layered several times in a process known as compound or serpentine layering. Climbing plants such as clematis, wisteria and grapevines lend themselves to this treatment.

Step-by-Step

AERIAL LAYERING

1 Choose a healthy shoot. Make a 45° slice about a third of the way through the stem with a sharp knife such as a budding knife or a secateur blade.

2 Gently lift open the cut, taking care not to break it. Push some sphagnum moss or coir peat into the split.

3 Wrap a plastic bag around the moss to hold it in place.

4 Secure it with ties at each end. When the roots are visible through the bag, detach the stem from the parent and put the new plant into its own position in the garden.

Aerial layering

Plants can also be encouraged to form roots through a process known as aerial layering or marcotting, which encourages a branch to form roots but without bending it down to the ground.

To make an aerial layer select a healthy stem or mature shoot around 30–60 cm long but don't remove it from the plant. Use a sharp knife (budding or grafting knife) or a secateur blade to cut half way through the stem below a node to reveal a section of the cambium layer.

Wedge the wounded stem open with a small stick such as a matchstick, dust it with hormone rooting powder or gel and then pack around the wound with moistened sphagnum moss or coir peat. The moss or peat should be damp but not overly wet. To finish your aerial layer, wrap the area in plastic and tie the bundle top and bottom with budding or other tape. It will resemble a bonbon.

Over time roots form around the layered area and the branch can be detached by cutting below the layer (that is cutting on the trunk side of the new roots) and replanted elsewhere. Allow three to six months for the aerial layer to form roots although some plants may form roots within weeks.

Plants that respond well to aerial layering include magnolias, fig trees (both edible and native), citrus, some conifers, banskias and any plants that naturally form aerial roots.

Other ways to propagate plants

Growing cuttings and dividing or layering plants are the easiest methods to propagate plants for home gardeners. However, there are other specialist techniques available that are often used by commercial plant propagators. These include budding, grafting and micro-propagation.

Budding and grafting are used to propagate plants that are grown on rootstocks such as fruit trees, many ornamental trees, roses and some Australian native plants. It is a specialised job that involves taking a small piece of one plant and bringing its cambium layer into contact with that of another plant.

Micro-propagation, also known as tissue culture, is employed to propagate some hard-to-grow plants including orchids, but requires specialist equipment, temperature control and high levels of hygiene for success.

This form of propagation uses a small piece of plant to grow more plants. This can be a piece of plant tissue or even a few cells. The cells are encouraged to divide and grow by plant hormones. They are usually grown on agar in sterile flasks or dishes.

RIGHT Magnolias are grown by a variety of propagation methods, including aerial layering and from cuttings, but some hybrids are also sold as grafted plants.

CHAPTER 5

Transplanting

Why do I need to read this chapter?

- 🌿 To decide whether or not to transplant a plant.

- 🌿 For tips on how best to move a plant.

- 🌿 To learn how to look after a transplant.

Weighing up the risks

We had a friend, a good gardener, who swore that every plant in her garden had been moved at least once. She said, proudly, that her plants shook with fear when they saw her with the spade in her hand. Her garden was full of healthy, well-grown plants, which is living proof that it is possible to move plants from one position to another and have them survive and even thrive.

Of course, there are always risks, and moving a plant, even a smallish one, can be a lot of work. Quite often transplanted plants suffer setbacks when being moved and there is always the chance that they will not survive. Other setbacks may include stunted growth, lack of flowers or fruit for several seasons, defoliation or broken or damaged branches.

If it's an unsuccessful transplant, the repercussions can be felt for many years. After an extreme heatwave period, a gardener reported that large shrubs he had transplanted more than a decade before had perished while nearby plants of the same variety that had not been moved survived the heat unscathed.

So there are several questions you need to ask yourself before you reach for the spade to dig up a plant and move it. The first and probably most important is: Why are you doing this? Also ask: Is the plant common and easily replaced with another? Can it be propagated? What happens to the plant if it isn't moved? Will removing it ruin your existing garden?

The desire to move plants is often brought on when you sell and move to a new garden. Gardeners on the move don't want to leave their plants behind, particularly plants to which they have a sentimental attachment.

If a plant is going to be destroyed by an extension, new construction or by land clearing you may think that it is worth trying to save it, but it is still important to look at the time and effort that are going to be involved and to assess whether the outcome is likely to be satisfactory and worth the effort.

A word on weight

As you'd expect, the larger and more established the plant, the more difficult it is to move. To move a small plant, all that's required is a spade or a trowel. Large plants are best moved with the aid of some form of mechanical equipment, such as a small excavator.

If your plant is relatively small— that is, under 1 m tall and wide—and particularly if it hasn't been in the ground for very long, then moving it will not be a very hard task. However, plants that are larger than 1 m high or wide, with substantial root systems, will require much more effort. Even moderately sized trees with their root

Think before you dig

Before you decide to dig up a plant and move it, run through this checklist to help you to assess whether the plant should be moved or not.

- How valuable is this plant to me?
- Can it be replaced?
- Can I simply take a cutting, divide or collect seeds?
- How tall is it?
- How big is the root ball?
- Do I need special equipment to move or transport this plant?
- What costs are involved?
- Can I find a new position for this plant?
- Can I dig a hole that's deep enough to accommodate the size of the root ball?
- How long before it can be replanted?
- Can I store it easily before it is replanted?
- Can I give it ongoing care?

LEFT Begin the process by digging a trench around the outer perimeter of the root ball.

Water regularly with a seaweed solution, concentrating on the root area inside the trench. This treatment encourages the plant to develop a smaller but sustaining root system that will be easier to transplant.

Preparing the planting hole

To reduce the risk of transplant shock, it is best to have a new planting hole already dug and prepared before you remove your plant from its original position. The new planting hole should easily contain the root ball, so dig it as deep as the root ball and about twice as wide. The extra width allows you to fully prepare the soil and to manoeuvre the plant with ease.

Also check drainage to avoid potential root rot. Poorly drained soils hold water around the root ball that can encourage fungal pathogens to flourish. Diseases that may occur include armillaria and phytophthora. For full details on how to dig a planting hole see 'How to plant a plant', page 20.

system and ball of soil can weigh a tonne or more.

When assessing the spread of a root system, remember that the root system will be wider than the above ground growth. It may not, however, be very deep. Root systems are often a metre or more in width, but only 30–60 cm deep. This can equate to a lot of weight, though, so don't overestimate your lifting abilities. Have extra help on hand and materials, such as a tarpaulin, to support the root system.

Getting ready

To begin the transplant process, dig a trench around the outer perimeter of the root ball. This severs roots and encourages the plant to form new feeder roots at the severance point.

Fill the trench with sand or a coarse, well-drained garden mix. If possible, make this the first step in your transplanting preparation, filling the trench at least 6–12 weeks before the actual move.

Tip Before you contemplate a transplant, dig a small trial hole in the new position to the depth required to check soil conditions before you embark on digging a large hole.

What you need to dig a large hole

The basic tools and materials needed are a sharp spade, a tarpaulin (to hold excavated soil) and a hose or source of water. You may also need a crowbar to remove large rocks from the hole. You also need compost and other organic matter to improve the planting soil.

To assess how large the planting hole needs to be, measure the size of the root ball if the plant has already been dug, or estimate its size if it is still in the original site—if this is the case, you may need to adjust the hole once the plant is dug up. The hole you need to dig may be 20–80 cm or more in depth. This means you may be digging into subsoil or even rock.

As you dig, keep the rich topsoil separate from any subsoil, putting it to one side of the hole. Poor quality subsoil may be best discarded and replaced with a good quality landscape or potting mix or with lots of extra compost and other organic matter, which is added to your topsoil.

If you strike rock or poor subsoil while digging and discover that you can't dig a hole that is deep enough to contain the transplant's root ball, reconsider the transplant, look for a new planting site or consider planting into a raised bed.

LEFT Every plant in this magnificent garden was transplanted from a garden ear-marked for bulldozing.
RIGHT To check that the soil drains well, dig a test hole, fill with water and time how long until it has drained away.

Checking drainage

If you can dig deeply enough to accommodate the transplanted root ball, it is still necessary to check how well the hole drains before you put the transplant into position. Heavy or clay soils may drain poorly and require some form of remedial treatment before planting occurs.

To check the drainage of any hole you dig, fill the hole with water and time how long the water takes to drain from the hole. Ideally the water should drain away in an hour or two. If it takes

longer than this, and particularly if it is still there after eight hours, your soil needs to be improved before it is used for planting by digging in gypsum and organic matter.

If the soil is very fast draining sandy soil, incorporate organic matter and water-holding crystals into the base of the hole and into the backfill before it is reused around the plant.

Removing the plant

Before you dig up the plant, mark or note its orientation so you know which part faced north. A good way to do this is to tie some coloured tags to the north-facing side of the plant. To reduce plant stress when you replant, orient the plant so the same part of the plant faces north as it did in its original location.

When you are ready to move the plant, return to the trench you dug earlier, dig it deeper, digging under the root ball (usually about a spade's depth or around 30–40 cm).

Remove the plant and carefully drop it on to a tarpaulin or into a wheelbarrow to transport it to its new location. If the plant is too large for you to lift in one go, lift part of it, slip a tarpaulin under the root ball, then lift the other side and drag it.

Tip Handle the transplant by its root ball, not its trunk, as the trunks are more easily broken.

Make sure the branches are secure during the move. If they are likely to be damaged, wrap or tie them up with a rope. If the plant is large with a heavy root ball, call in some mechanical assistance. Use a small bobcat or digger to help lift and then transfer the transplant to its new location. It is possible to hire a small digger that can be operated by a home gardener. Large equipment, such as a bobcat, are hired with an operator. As well as paying for the operator and machine, you may also need to cover transport or 'float' costs.

Storing a transplant

When transplanting, you would ideally have the hole in the new spot ready. If this is not possible, you will need to wrap the root ball and its surrounding soil in hessian or a tarpaulin.

Alternatively, you could store the plant in a temporary position. This is done by covering the roots with soil or putting the plant into a pot or other container. If the plant is being stored in a container, remove soil from around its roots, trim any damaged roots and put the plant into a pot that's larger than the root ball. Use potting mix, ensuring there are no air pockets around the roots. Firm the potting mix in around the roots and water well.

LEFT Ensure the roots of the transplant are well-protected.

Planting a transplant

Once you have the hole prepared, it's time to get the transplanted plant into the ground. Water the plant well before it is replanted. As with planting potted plants, wetting or soaking the root ball in a seaweed solution can reduce transplant stress.

If you have had the root ball wrapped or potted, remove the outer layer or container and examine the root ball. Use sharp secateurs or a pruning saw to trim any damaged or spiralling roots and lightly prune the root ball so that it comfortably fits into its new home. This pruning also encourages new root growth.

If you are moving your plant to a totally new area with different soil it is also best to remove all existing soil from around the roots before replanting. Do this by gently hosing the soil away from the root ball. Soil incompatibility may affect water absorption and the successful growth of the plant in its new location.

With the root ball prepared, gently lower the plant into its new position, orientating the plant so that it faces in the same direction as it did in its old position. Adjust the depth of the hole if necessary by digging it out more or replacing some of the excavated soil.

It may also be necessary to further trim the root ball to help fit the plant into its new position. The top of the root ball should sit at the top of the soil and the plant should be centred in the planting hole.

Planting at the right level

Use the soil you removed from the hole to fill in around the root ball. Firm the soil as you go. When about three quarters of the root ball is planted, water the plant well, adding extra soil over any exposed roots. This is done to remove air pockets and to ensure that all the roots are well surrounded by soil.

Continue backfilling around the roots until the entire root ball is covered with soil. Don't mound soil over the original surface or around the trunk. Firm around the surface and water it again well, topping up any soil as needed.

Finish the planting by creating a saucer-shaped depression around the tree to funnel water towards the root system. Cover the soil with a fine layer of compost or well-rotted manure and a 3–5 cm layer of coarse mulch.

If you have planted a large tree or shrub, particularly in an exposed position, it may be necessary to stake it to reduce wind rock. This is a condition where the wind that is buffeting the plant constantly interferes with root establishment and regrowth. Existing roots are disturbed as the plant moves and any new roots that form are damaged. Use three firm stakes. Two-metre long wooden stakes that are 50 mm square are needed to support a large transplant. Take care to drive the stakes firmly into the ground (to a depth of at least 50 cm and beyond the root ball), ensuring it is deeper than

ABOVE To help get the depth of the plant in the hole right, lay a stake across the top of the root ball and the hole as a guide.

the root ball. Secure the plant to the three stakes with a broad, soft material such as jute webbing to avoid damage to the trunk. Do not use wire or other material that may cut into the bark.

Tip Plant growth is slow or even dormant during winter, making it the ideal time to move an established plant. However, it's best to avoid very cold or icy periods.

Step-by-Step

HOW TO MOVE A SHRUB

1 Slice all the way around the shrub with a spade, about 30 cm out from the trunk. Cut through any roots with a spade, or loppers. Dig under the root ball with the spade and lever the plant out.

2 Dig a new hole for the plant that's the same depth as the root ball and at least as big. Position the plant in the new hole and turn it until it is facing the same direction as it did in the old hole.

3 Backfill around the plant, pushing the soil right down to the bottom of the hole. Don't cover the root ball with soil—it should be at the same level as the surrounding ground. Finally, water well, mulch and water again. Continue to inspect and water as the plant re-establishes.

Additionally, a screen of hessian or shadecloth may be needed to shade new transplants from extreme heat and protect from cold or hot winds.

As part of ongoing care for the transplant, regularly check stakes and ties. Replace any that have become worn and loosen any that are becoming too tight or causing damage. Ensure there are no insects clustering under the plant tie. Remove covers and protection when the plant is well established in its new location.

Looking after transplants

The time it takes for a transplanted plant to re-establish in a new location can vary from weeks to months depending on how quickly it can develop a new root system. For some plants, it takes years to recover their original health after transplanting.

To reduce transplant shock, water the plant regularly with a seaweed solution. It is a good idea to apply the seaweed solution every week for several weeks, reducing frequency as the plant becomes established. It is also necessary to water the transplant once or twice a week so that it doesn't become dried out. In hot or windy weather, more frequent watering may be needed to prevent stress.

To assess the plant's water needs feel the soil—it should be moist around the root ball—and examine the foliage looking for signs of wilting. If the transplant does dry out, soak it thoroughly. If the water isn't absorbed and runs off, rather than soaks in, water over the soil area with a soil-wetting agent to aid water penetration.

Once the transplant shows signs of new growth, scatter organic fertiliser such as blood and bone, pelletised chicken manure or slow-release fertiliser prills around the root system.

Begin to cut back on watering as the plant re-establishes, but do this gradually and in tune with the needs of your plant and its new situation.

Tip If you can't find a soft broad material to use as a plant tie, use rope threaded through a length of garden hose. Position the hose around the trunk.

Signs of transplant shock

It is normal for plants to suffer when transplanted. Old leaves may become yellow or fall while buds or flowers may drop. Leaves and shoots may droop or wilt, particularly on hot or sunny days. Provided wilting recovers when the plant is watered and new growth appears to replace discarded leaves, your plant is probably going to be okay in its new home.

If your transplant shows signs of dieback, leaf death or persistent wilting it may require extra attention. These symptoms may indicate root death due to transplant damage, drying out or over-watering. Adjust watering if over- or under-watering is occurring and treat root problems with a fungicide drench.

Phosacid is a phosphorus acid-based fungicide that can combat root rot problems. Apply the fungicide according to the instructions on the container. To help the plant to regenerate, encourage new shoots by giving the plant a light prune. Alleviate heat stress by providing some temporary shade. This can take the form of a shadecloth cover or screen.

Stressed plants are vulnerable to pest attacks. A pest control tablet containing Imidacloprid inserted around the root system can control pest problems. Follow instructions on the packet for application rates and methods.

RIGHT Use a soft plant tie to secure the stem to its supporting stake.

Moving pots

Moving a potted plant may seem like a very easy thing to do: you simply pick up the plant pot and all and move it to the new location. Pots, after all, are supposed to be portable. However, if you are moving a pot any distance, and particularly when you are moving house, there are issues to consider.

Old pots may be fragile and easily broken. Plastic pots that have been outside exposed to light may have become brittle and can disintegrate.

Plants that have been growing in a pot for a long time may be past their best or may have grown through the base of the pot and into the ground below so that lifting them is difficult and can damage the plant. If the plant has outgrown its pot or the pot is damaged and unsuited to being moved, consider bare-rooting the potted plant for the move and re-potting it into a new pot at the new location.

To bare-root a potted plant, simply take it out of its pot, remove the potting mix from around the root system and wrap the roots in moist sphagnum moss or fresh, moist potting mix and plastic. A large plastic bin liner may give temporary protection for a bare-rooted plant.

As well as assessing the container and root system, also examine the plant itself carefully. Potted plants may also contain weeds, which you risk spreading to a new environment, or they may harbour insects such as ants, snails or slaters. Bushy plants may even contain a bird's nest, so carefully examine each pot plant to assess its suitability for moving. To make sure you've considered everything, follow the checklist on page 74.

Moving day

If the pot and plant get the tick of approval and are safe to move, consider how you are going to physically move each pot. If you are moving house, make sure you check that your removalist will move pots, that they are included on the quote and that none get left behind.

If you are moving pots yourself, do it in a van so that both loading and unloading are easy and that any mess that's caused can be readily cleaned up. Placing potted plants inside a van also reduces the damage that can be caused by having them blown about in the wind in an open trailer or by being squeezed into a car seat or a car boot.

Finally, if you are moving to a different climate zone, remember the potted plant may not be suitable for the new climate. It may be better to give it away to a friend or neighbour, or to sell it in the pre-move garage sale.

LEFT Buy or hire a trolley to assist you with moving large pots, as these items are heavy.
RIGHT Protect a bare-rooted plant with sphagnum moss and a plastic bag.

Transplant Q and A

Lots of questions arise when we contemplate transplanting a tree or shrub in our garden. Here are answers to some of the most commonly asked transplant questions.

What is the best time to do it?

It is best to transplant a plant when it is not actively growing, flowering or under stress. If the plant is naturally deciduous in autumn (that is, it loses its leaves and is bare during winter), then late autumn, winter or very early spring are ideal times to transplant even quite large trees and shrubs.

Late autumn through to early spring are also the best times of the year to transplant an evergreen plant. Although evergreen plants are not completely dormant in winter, most are in less active growth and less likely to come under transplant stress. If an evergreen

Moving a potted plant checklist

- Is the new position suitable for this plant?
- Is the new climate suitable for this plant?
- Is the root system contained in the pot?
- Is the pot intact or damaged?
- Does the pot contain weeds or pests?
- Is the plant itself healthy?
- Can I lift this plant?

plant flowers during winter (such as a camellia), wait until it has finished or nearly finished its flowering then move it before it puts on a spurt of new growth.

For any plant, transplanting in summer can lead to stress. This is because the plant's damaged or disturbed roots cannot bring moisture from the soil to the leaves efficiently. Extra shade, misting and regular watering are all required to keep a transplant going during hot weather. If you have no choice but to transplant at a less than optimum time, ensure your plant is given extra care and protection during hot periods.

To prune or not to prune?

There is no straightforward answer to this question. Many variables need to be taken into account.

Often plants need to be pruned just so they can be transported and handled with ease. Also, if the plant is being moved in winter, at a time when it would normally be pruned, pruning before moving is sensible. If the plant has lots of flowering growth on it when it is to be moved this should be pruned away. Dead or diseased wood should also be pruned.

Pruning reduces stress on the root system, so it is a sensible precaution during warmer weather to reduce moisture loss. However, at other times pruning may not be needed, so don't prune unnecessarily or you may ruin the shape of the plant you are moving.

ABOVE Pruning a rose before transplant may not be necessary; it depends on the time of year.

Can I move a native plant?

The transplanting of native plants has always been seen as a tricky task, doomed to failure. However, as more mature native plants are planted in gardens and the broader landscape, it is apparent that it is possible to relocate native plants, including eucalypts.

Among the biggest native trees to be relocated are native figs (*Ficus macrophylla*), used in large landscaping projects. Some have been so big they've been moved by a semi-trailer, or even barge, to their new growing sites. Large bottle trees (*Brachychiton rupestris*) have also been successfully transplanted.

In most cases, though, the risk of plant death far outweighs the effort needed to relocate a large native plant, so it is rarely worth the effort. Smaller new plants are a better option as they quickly outgrow a large transplant.

Planting advanced shrubs and trees

If you are moving house, transplanting is not your only option. In terms of preparation, buying an advanced plant is a similar undertaking to shifting a plant to a new location.

Advanced plants are those that have been grown at a nursery for several years so they are a mature size. They are usually grown in large pots or root control bags but they may also be grown in the ground and dug up.

The benefit of buying advanced plants, especially for a new garden, is that they can bring instant maturity. Large advanced trees provide shade and add a sense of scale to a new garden, while buying large shrubs for an advanced hedge can also provide instant shelter and screening for an exposed site.

If you don't want to wait years for small plants to grow, then advanced plants can be the answer. In buying a tree or shrub that's already reached maturity, you also know the shape and size of the tree you are planting.

The downsides of buying advanced plants are that they are expensive and require special care after planting to ensure that they survive.

If you decide to plant advanced plants in your garden, it's a good idea to consider buying direct from an advanced tree specialist. You may even want to engage the services of

ABOVE These trees have been grown in the ground for several years and are ready for transplanting.

a landscape designer or contractor to oversee the job. The cost of using a professional may only be a small expense on top of the actual cost of a number of advanced plants.

Specialist growers can provide delivery and planting services. If you want to do the planting yourself, they

can provide information about what needs to be done before your advanced plant arrives, including the size of planting hole needed, the optimum site and soil requirements, and advice on ongoing care. For general advice on what may be involved, see 'Planting a transplant' on page 69.

CHAPTER 6

How to grow a lawn

Why do I need to read this chapter?

- 🪣 To find out how to plant different types of lawns.
- 🪣 For tips on getting your lawn to grow perfectly.
- 🪣 To get smart ideas for watering and maintenance.

Growing a green space

Lawns fall in and out of fashion, often reflecting prevailing water restrictions and concerns about our environmental footprint. But a lawn is a major asset in a garden as it provides a safe area for recreation—from playing games to relaxing—as well as being a green link that unifies the garden.

A lawn will always need mowing, which usually means using fossil fuels (unless you have a push mower), but there are positive environmental effects to be gained from an established lawn that can offset the use of fossil fuels.

Areas of lawn around a house are cooler than hard paving and can help reduce the amount of energy needed to cool a house over summer. Lawns also reduce run-off as they allow water to percolate into the soil. Selecting the appropriate variety for your needs and climate will reduce the amount of water the lawn requires, thereby reducing its strain on the environment.

Turf or seed?

There are many ways to start a lawn. Depending on the variety you want to grow, the season and how quickly you want a green sward, you can establish lawns by planting seed, sprigs or runners or by just rolling out turf.

The slowest but cheapest method to grow many varieties of lawns is by sowing seed. Turf is the most expensive way to start a lawn but it gives instant results. (See 'How to lay turf', page 80.) Sprigs or runners can reduce the cost of turf but do take time and effort to both plant and establish.

To help you decide which variety of lawn to grow study the 'Grass types' table on page 82 to see which variety suits your climate and needs.

From seed is the cheapest way to grow a lawn but not all lawn varieties are available as seed. The savings and ease of sowing seed must be weighed up against the time required to get a seed-grown lawn established, which can be several months.

Preparation

Before sowing lawn seed or laying turf spend time preparing the soil. It should be level, free of lumps, rocks and debris and of a good texture so seed can germinate and grow and turf can establish.

Start off by removing any existing grass and weeds from the area. This can be done manually using a turf cutter or a spade, or by spraying the area with a glyphosate-based herbicide.

Cultivate the soil so it has a loose, crumbly texture then rake it over vigorously to remove stones, unbroken clods and roots. To provide a well-

TOP Rake the seed bed so it is level and clear of stones or clods.

ABOVE A section of existing turf can be used to patch up any bare spots in a large area of lawn.

drained layer of soil for the seed bed or to lay turf on, invest in a load of organic soil mix, also sold as turf underlay. Spread this to a depth of at least 5 cm over the lawn area and level.

Turf underlay is available from most landscape suppliers and can be bought by the cubic metre.

To estimate how much is required for your lawn area, measure the length and width of the area in metres then multiply by .05 m to allow for 5 cm coverage. For example, if your lawn

Step-by-Step

HOW TO SOW LAWN SEED

1 Prepare the site and rake the soil until it's fine, crumbly and level.

2 To ensure even coverage, scatter half the seed one way and half at right angles to it. If you are sowing a large area, it's worth using a seed spreader to ensure even distribution.

3 Lightly rake over the site so most of the seeds are covered with soil. Tamp it down with the back of a rake so it is firm.

4 Water in, then water regularly to keep moist. Seedlings should appear in 14 days.

Other options for creating a lawn

If you have a small budget and large areas to cover, use sprigs, which are small sections of grass with roots and leaves, and are treated like cuttings.

Make sprigs by cutting small pieces of turf from your lawn or buying a few rolls of turf and dividing these large sections into small pieces of stem. Each piece should have roots and leaves.

To plant, use a spade to make a flap in the soil. Bury the roots and half the leaves, covering firmly with the soil. Plant sprigs 7 cm apart in rows 5–10 cm apart across damaged areas. Apply slow-release fertiliser and keep weed free as the sprigs take off.

BELOW Break up a small roll of turf or try digging pieces from an existing lawn to form sprigs for a cheap way to start a new lawn.

area measures 5 x 4 m, multiply their product by 0.05 m to get the amount of turf underlay required, in this case, 1 cubic metre.

Broadcast a slow-release lawn starter fertiliser and water gently. You and your garden are now ready for seed to be sown or turf to be laid.

Step-by-Step

HOW TO LAY TURF

1   Remove any debris and then level the site.

2   Spread a 5 cm layer of top dressing and tamp it down. You can use a flat board, the back of a rake or, for a small area, simply tread all over the site.

3   Apply lawn starter fertiliser at the recommended rate. For even distribution over large areas, use a spreader.

4   Turf comes in rolls 50 cm wide x 2 m long. Turf should not be left rolled for longer than a day as it soon yellows and dies, so organise delivery on the day you're ready to lay the turf.

5   Lay turf, starting along one edge, ideally butting against a hard surface such as a path or wall. If you're laying turf on a slope, the turf should be laid across the slope rather than down it. Lay it in a brick pattern and make a tight join with the adjacent piece of turf. Firm as you go by tamping the turf down with the back of a metal rake.

6   Sprinkle a fine layer of lawn top dressing over the surface and brush it into the joins with a stiff brush to fill any gaps. Give the new lawn a good soak then continue watering regularly—two or three times a week—until the turf has rooted. Mow after roots are established and the lawn is growing well.

Ongoing care for your lawn

Lawn care revolves around weeding, watering, mowing and fertilising. If you want an immaculate, green, weed-free lawn, spend time each week caring for and maintaining your lawn. If you are happy to have a patch of grass that's green and relatively weed free, you can cut back the time spent on maintenance. Here is a guide to the basics of lawn care.

Get fertilising in spring

As soon as the grass starts to regrow after winter, it is time to fertilise your lawn. To reduce nutrient run-off, use a slow-release product that provides a steady feed to the roots as they begin to absorb nutrients. The ideal time to apply fertiliser is after rain when the soil is moist. Use a fertiliser spreader—either hand held or wheeled—to ensure an even distribution of fertiliser across your lawn. For newly laid lawns, select a lawn starter product but for established lawns use your preferred lawn food. Lawns are fed in spring and late summer or early autumn in most areas but require more frequent feeding in the tropics where wet season rains and fast growth quickly leach away nutrients from the soil.

TOP An even green lawn unifies the look of a garden and provide space to relax.
ABOVE Use a hand-held fertiliser spreader to evenly distribute fertiliser over your lawn.

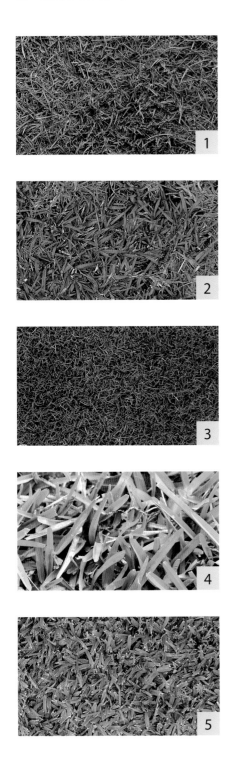

Grass types

If you are planting a new lawn you have many options. If you are planning to grow a hard-wearing, drought-tolerant lawn, running varieties are a more waterwise choice than cool season, clumping grasses, such as rye or fescue.

Type of grass	Climate	Start with
1 Kikuyu	Warm (tropical, subtropical, temperate, inland)	Seed, runners or turf
2 Small-leafed carpet grass	Warm to tropical (tropical, subtropical, inland)	Turf
3 Couch	Warm to tropical	Turf
4 Soft-leafed buffalo (also sold as St Augustine grass)	All areas	Turf
5 Buffalo (also sold as St Augustine grass)	All areas but mainly grown in warm, coastal areas	Turf
6 Durban grass (also sold as Sweet Smother)	Warm	Turf
7 Perennial rye	Cool to cool temperate areas	Seed or turf (often in a mixture with other cool season lawn grasses)
8 Kentucky blue grass	Cool	Seed or turf
9 Fescue, tall fescue	Cool climates	Seed, turf
10 Temple grass, zoysia, empire grass	Tropical to temperate (not frost tolerant)	Sprigs, turf

Comment

Dies off in dry times, but regrows quickly after rain. Growth slows and lawn browns in cold weather. This is the cheapest of all lawn grasses and also the most vigorous and invasive. Needs frequent mowing in summer. Some shade tolerance, but best in full sun. An ideal choice for a lawn that receives hard wear.

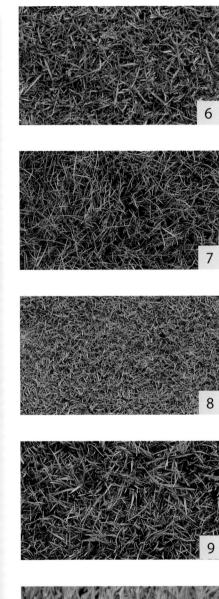

Slow-growing lawn grass that tolerates shade and acid soils.

Fine lawn grass with low water needs. Many named varieties, some of which produce a very fine lawn. Drought tolerant once established. Most varieties brown off in winter. Can be invasive. Grows best in full sun. May be closely mowed for a fine finish. A good choice for a show lawn in a warm climate.

Broad-leafed, warm-season grass. Many named varieties. Some varieties are slow growing, others have good shade tolerance. Leaf blade width varies and can affect overall lawn appearance. Good drought tolerance once established. Not frost tolerant.

Broad-leafed warm season grass now replaced in the marketplace by finer-leafed forms sold as soft-leafed buffalo (see above). Can cause skin irritation.

A broad-leafed warm climate grass with good shade tolerance. Suitable for planting under trees. May be difficult to source.

All-purpose grass, often sold in lawn seed mixes. Requires summer moisture to keep green. Good winter colour. Good shade tolerance. Can be sown to provide winter colour in warm season turf varieties.

A clumping lawn grass for cool climates. Not drought tolerant. Keep well watered and well fertilised. To reduce stress mow no closer than 8–10 cm.

Clumping grass that maintains green year round. Requires water in dry times. As a clumping grass, this lawn does not self-repair if it dies.

A slow-growing lawn grass to around 10 cm high. Can be left unmown to create an informal mounded ground cover appearance, or mown to as low as 5 mm for a traditional lawn. Good drought tolerance once established. Can tolerate some shade. Salt tolerant. Not good for high-traffic areas.

Mowing while it's growing

Lawn mowing is more than a chore designed to make the grass look neat. Regular mowing encourages lawns to thicken up. Don't cut your lawn too closely, however, or it will become weakened and quickly infiltrated by weeds. Longer leaves also help protect the lawn from heat. Raise the mower blades so that lawn is 2.5–3.5 cm high after cutting. Don't mow wet grass and make sure your blades are sharp and cutting effectively. Blunt or damaged blades rip rather than cut the lawn. For details on caring for lawn mowers and mower maintenance, see Chapter 10, page 164.

Grass clippings can be left on the lawn or removed in a catcher and used to compost as mulch. Left on the lawn, the clippings quickly break down, returning nourishment to the soil. A mulching mower speeds up the process and removes the clippings, which can look unsightly.

If you are using a line trimmer or whipper snipper to mow grass in hard-to-reach spots, such as around trunks, take care not to let the string bite into the bark. This damages trees and shrubs and the wounds can provide an entry point for disease. Keep away from trunks or exposed roots, or protect them with a guard.

When mowing, always wear enclosed shoes and long pants to avoid injury. Also pick up any debris that may be on your lawn before you get started to prevent accidents.

OPPOSITE Mow your lawns regularly while they are growing to keep them thick and healthy. Wear appropriate footwear and clothing to prevent accidents.

TOP Adjust the height of the mower according to the height you want the finished cut to be.

ABOVE A hand or push mower is an efficient and environmentally friendly way to mow small areas of grass.

RIGHT Use a line trimmer to keep the lawn from invading garden beds.

Reducing compaction

To aerate, drive the tines of a garden fork into the compacted area. Push back on the handle and pull it through at a 30° angle to lift and crack the soil.

Aerating

Over time, as people play, walk or park their vehicles on it, lawns become compacted. Grass doesn't like growing on compacted soils so it may become thin or bare in these spots. Weeds are not as fussy and quickly move in. Bindii in particular thrives in compacted soils. To fix compaction, drive a garden fork into the soil to make holes. If you have a large area that's compacted, hire a lawn aerator to make the task easier. After aerating spread a fine layer of sand or a top dressing mix.

Dealing with weeds

Weeds are the bane of a lawn-proud gardener's life. They interfere with the overall look of the lawn and, if the lawn is not growing strongly, can overrun it. To reduce weeds, keep the lawn growing vigorously with regular feeding through the growing period (a slow-release lawn food applied in spring and summer is ideal). Give the lawn a deep, soaking water at least once a week and mow regularly to encourage strong leaf growth.

Weeds, particularly flat weeds such as dandelion and cat's ear, prosper in lawns where the soil pH is acidic. Apply lime to lawns to raise the soil pH in acidic soils. Compacted soils, which are difficult for lawn grasses to grow in, are also readily colonised by low-growing weeds such as bindii (see 'Aerating' at left for tips on dealing with compacted soils).

Don't wait until your lawn is bare and weedy—fix small bare spots quickly to avoid big problems later. Either patch them with sprigs or runners from elsewhere or, if you have a seeded lawn, patch with lawn seed (see the step-by-step advice for how to do this on page 79).

Mossy lawns

Lawns that are shaded or poorly drained can develop moss. Moss can be removed in the short term with a moss killer, but long term the only way to dissuade moss is to let more light into the area and to redirect excess water.

Prune back overhanging branches and shrubs that are encroaching on the lawn to allow more direct light. Investigate surface and subsurface drains to deal with run-off.

BELOW Use excess turf to patch bare areas. Cut the grass into small sections (top); before planting (bottom).

Watering

Lawns respond quickly to water whether it is from irrigation or a good downpour by producing lots of green, leafy growth. Make sure all water can quickly penetrate your soil by regularly aerating compacted soil (see 'Aerating' opposite) and by applying soil-wetting agents if the soil is water repellent. In dry summer areas where water restrictions ban the watering of lawns, consider using tank water to keep your lawn green. If there is no water available, avoid walking on dry grass. It will revive quickly when the rain returns.

Lawn repair

Lawns need to be dethatched—that is, the dead grass and debris that build up within the leafy growth of the lawn must be removed.

From time to time, lawns should be top dressed with a coarse sandy material. This is done to level lawns and can also be done after aerating to keep the aerated holes open. It doesn't have to be done annually.

To keep lawns green all year round, regularly re-seed any worn patches and oversow patchy lawns in winter with a cool season lawn grass seed such as perennial rye or a clover and rye blend.

RIGHT Install a tank to provide water for lawns and gardens.
FAR RIGHT A sprinkler on a timer is the easiest and most efficient way to water lawns.

Step-by-Step

TOP DRESSING A LAWN

1 Sprinkle top dressing over the lawn to a depth of about 25 mm, adding more to dips or hollows.

2 With a metal rake, spread the top dressing out evenly. Make sure that the tips of the grass blades are still poking through the top dressing.

3 Water well. Leave the top dressing to settle for three to four weeks and repeat, if necessary, until the surface is level.

Other options

Not every part of the garden is suitable for growing lawn. Many of the difficulties encountered with maintaining a garden stem from attempts at growing grass where it won't perform well. If an area is shaded, has root competition from nearby trees, is extremely steep, uneven or rocky or is difficult to access for ongoing maintenance such as mowing and watering, don't plant lawn. Instead select another method to cover the soil such as alternative ground cover plants or some form of mulch.

For ground-hugging plants that act as a lawn alternative, select low-growing or spreading plants that form roots from their nodes to give a dense, mat-like coverage.

 Tip   Unlike grass, most groundcover plants tolerate only occasional foot traffic, so provide stepping stones or a path if access is needed.

OPPOSITE Round stepping stones allow access across this dichondra lawn.

Ajuga, bugle (*Ajuga reptans*) Shade to part shade, cool to subtropical climates

Australian native violet (*Viola hederacea*) Shade, all climates

Chamomile (*Chamaemelum nobile* 'Treneague') Shade, cool climates

Kidney weed (*Dichondra repens*) Sun to shade, all climates

Mondo grass (*Ophiopogon japonicus* 'Nana'—sold as Mini Mondo) Full sun to shade, all climates

Thyme, lemon-scented thyme (*Thymus serpyllum*, *T.* x *citriodorus*) Full sun, cool climates

Step-by-Step

LEVELLING A LAWN

Uneven lawns can be hard work: they are harder to walk on; dips and hollows can fill with long grass; lumps and humps make mowing difficult, and compaction in high traffic areas makes it harder for the grass to grow. If the problem is too big to be solved by applying top dressing, the best way to fix these problems is to adjust the soil level beneath the lawn.

1 Assess the area of the hollow or hump and slice through the turf around the perimeter.

2 Slice beneath the turf with a spade and lift up the grass. Place it on a tarpaulin to one side. If the grass is in good condition you may be able to peel back the sections.

3 Dig or fork over the ground to break up any compaction. Add or remove soil as required to obtain the correct level.

4 Tread over the surface to lightly firm it down, then use your rake to break up the surface and ensure the grass roots come in contact with the soil.

5 Replace the turf, butting the edges closely together. Bare patches can be filled with sprigs or part of a roll of turf.

6 Tamp turf down with the back of a rake or by lightly walking over it. Top dress to fill in gaps and water well. Avoid walking on the area until it re-establishes.

Lawn or grass?

Do you have lawn or just grass? Although 'lawn' conjures up images of manicured, well-mown and well-maintained sward, in truth, they are virtually one and the same. Lawns are usually composed of just one variety, although some seed-grown lawns include a mixture of lawn grasses. So, if you want to turn grass into lawn, get out the lawn mower!

Seasonal lawn calendar

Spring

- Repair worn spots by re-seeding or patching.
- Relieve compaction by forking or aerating the lawn.
- Lightly top dress to fill holes made by aerating and to level lawns.
- To repair deep depressions, cut turf, fill and replace the turf.
- Treat or remove germinating weeds, especially flat weeds.
- Apply lawn food after rain or a deep watering and as soil temperatures warm.
- Mow regularly as growth resumes.

Summer

- If rain is scarce and water use restricted, allow warm-season grasses (such as running lawns) to brown off.
- Continue to use available water to maintain cool-season lawns.
- If there's enough rain or water available, water lawns at least once a week to maintain strong growth.
- Mow growing lawns regularly but don't scalp the lawn by mowing too close.
- Repair worn spots to stop weeds invading.
- Keep edges of lawns well trimmed to avoid runners invading garden beds and paths.

Autumn

- After rain, oversow warm-season lawn grasses (couch, soft-leafed buffalo, kikuyu) with perennial rye grass seed for winter colour.
- Repair worn patches in cool-season lawn by re-seeding.
- Scarify lawns where thatch has built up. To do this, drag a metal rake through the lawn to remove dead grass.
- Reduce mowing as temperatures cool.
- Fertilise cool-season lawns.

Winter

- Browning off of warm-season lawns is normal in winter especially after frost. Do not fertilise until weather warms.
- Reduce mowing as grass growth slows with cooler conditions and shorter days.
- Avoid walking on grass that's heavily frosted.
- Control weeds, especially bindii, which begin to grow in winter. Use a selective herbicide.
- Clover growth may increase in lawns. This can be left as it increases soil nitrogen or controlled by mowing or using selective herbicides.

How to water the lawn

Lawns grow best with deep soaking once or twice a week rather than a light sprinkle, which usually fails to wet the root zone. A sustained fall of rain is the best water for your garden but, when there's no rain about, extra irrigation is necessary to maintain green growing grass.

Running grasses such as couch, kikuyu and buffalo become dormant without regular water so, over dry summers, if you elect not to water these lawn grasses turn brown. The first rain, or a heavy watering, will kick them back into growth.

Cool-season lawn grasses, such as rye, tall fescue and Kentucky blue grass, which form clumps, die back over summer without regular watering.

To water lawns, and where water restrictions permit, set a hose with a

ABOVE Clover growth increases during winter but may be left as it increases soil nitrogen.

Note If any of your plants rely on run-off from your lawn watering, they will become stressed and may die if you stop irrigating your lawn. It will be necessary to individually water these plants during dry periods.

sprinkler attachment (use a timer to avoid wasting water) or use pop-up irrigation sprinklers through the lawn. These can be installed when the lawn is laid. A pop-up sprinkler system allows the grass to be mowed without interfering with the irrigation system. These sprinklers pop up due to water pressure when the irrigation system is switched on, then drop back down when the water is switched off.

After prolonged dry periods, soils may become water repellent, making it hard to get water to percolate down to root areas. The best way to overcome this is by applying a soil-wetting agent. Hose-on applicators make it an easy task.

In dry times, many gardeners use grey water to keep their lawn green. If you do this, keep in mind that most health restrictions require untreated grey water—the water from your washing machine or shower—to be delivered beneath the soil surface. Treated grey and black water (water from septic tanks that is fully processed) can be used on lawns.

To avoid unwanted build-ups of salts on the lawn, allow it to dry out between waterings with grey water and, if possible, intersperse grey water with rain or town water.

LEFT If you don't have a sprinkler and need to water with a hose, ensure you water each area thoroughly.

OPPOSITE Thyme may be used as an aromatic alternative to lawn in low-traffic areas.

CHAPTER 7

How to grow a hedge

Why do I need to read this chapter?

- To find out how to plant a hedge.

- To learn how to care for hedges.

- To discover the wide range of hedges you can create.

Hedging your bets

Hedges are more than a living fence. Not only do they create habitat for insects, birds and animals, they also provide climate control and add a sense of privacy.

The term 'hedge' may conjure up images of clipped conifer hedges around old-style houses or perhaps dense, gloomy laurel hedges of the kind you read about in thrillers and whodunnits. But a hedge can be big or small, green or coloured and composed of just about any type of plant you like. You can even plant a flowering hedge or include a productive hedge to extend your edible garden to your boundary.

Perhaps one of the best reasons to plant a hedge is because it is a structure you can grow yourself. If you start with cuttings, a hedge can be a cheap yet effective way to create fences, enclosures or internal screens. All you really need is patience.

Once your hedge is growing, you also need to undertake regular maintenance to keep it healthy. Hedges need to be pruned and shaped once or twice a year, or even more frequently, depending on the variety.

RIGHT Dense, clipped hedges such as this laurel hedge (*Prunus laurocerasus*) protect open areas from cold winds and create privacy.

How to plant

Many of the downsides of having a hedge are reduced by good soil preparation and planning. Before you plant, clear the area where the hedge is to be grown. Remove weeds, stumps and stones, and improve the soil with manure and well-rotted compost.

As part of the planning of the hedge, consider how you are going to give it ongoing care. If possible, run an irrigation line along the row of plants with drippers or micro-sprayers at each plant. If the hedge is in an area that's remote from a tap, consider using a temporary soaker hose or some kind of water well to keep the plants properly watered while they settle in. These can be homemade (for example a leaky bottle, as shown on page 141) or a commercial water-well product.

Planting and spacing

To ensure your hedge is planted in a straight line, and the plants are evenly spaced, measure out the length of the hedge by placing stakes at each end of the hedge. Run a string line between the two stakes for a planting guide.

The space allowed between each plant depends on the width of the plant as it grows, its rate of growth and how quickly you want your hedge to join up. Use the table on page 112 as a guide to the expected size of individual hedge plants. As a rule of thumb, space hedge plants at half their final width apart. For example, shrubs that grow

Pros and cons of a hedge

A hedge is an ongoing commitment, with many benefits to both the garden and the environment. Here's a list of the pros and cons you should familiarise yourself with before making a decision about whether or not to plant a hedge.

Pros	Cons
Hedges will:	Hedges will:
• extend your garden	• take years to establish, as they grow slowly and need to fill out as well as grow up
• complement the style and design of your house and garden, if chosen wisely	• be difficult to change or alter at a later date
• be a cheap addition to your garden, if established from cuttings	• be expensive if established from mature plants
• live for an extended period of time	• have uneven growth
• be of benefit to the environment	• require ongoing maintenance such as regular pruning
• provide wildlife habitat	

2 m wide can be spaced a metre apart but for faster coverage, plant them at 50–75 cm spacings, adjusting to accommodate the actual length of the hedge.

Quick calculation

There are two ways you can work out how many plants you will need: you can physically place pots or markers where the plant will grow, or you can do the calculation on paper. If your hedge is going to be 5 m long and you are growing dwarf lillypillies, which have a width of 1.5 m, you would ideally plant them 75 cm apart. However, to fit them evenly, position a hedge plant at each end and use six more plants to fill the space. That's eight plants in total. To space them evenly adjust the distances between

ABOVE Clipped hedges create formal patterns and shapes within a larger area.

each plant so they are around 65 cm apart (if you're really fussy, 62.5 cm).

If you do the maths first, you'll know how many you need before you get to the nursery. Always buy a couple more than you calculate you need so there are plants on hand if there's a casualty, you've miscalculated or if one of the plants is not well shaped. These extra plants can be grown in pots, ready for use as required, or planted elsewhere in the garden to be transplanted if needed.

To make sure you space your hedge plants evenly, use a measure—a length of timber or a stick cut to the right length makes a handy spacer while you are setting out your plants.

Before planting, set the hedge plants out in their allocated spot along the string line with a plant at each end of the hedge.

To plant, simply dig a hole that's the same depth as the root ball but a little wider. Take the hedge plant out of its pot and place it in the planting hole. Stake the plant if the hedge is exposed to strong winds. If it is in an area where it may be attacked by rabbits, wallabies or other pests, surround it with a protective barrier. This could be made from hessian, shadecloth or chicken wire wrapped around stakes. Alternatively, use a commercial product such as a grow bag.

Water the plants in well, firming into the soil. For more on how to plant, see page 20. Apply a controlled-release fertiliser. Finish off the planting with a layer of mulch around and between each plant. For more on fertilising and mulching see Chapter 9.

Uniformity

One of the joys of a hedge is that the plants are all of a uniform colour and shape. This uniform appearance is managed by pruning and shaping, but

ABOVE LEFT Use a string line as a guide to space plants in an orderly row.
ABOVE RIGHT Once planted, add a slow-release fertiliser and surround each plant with organic mulch, such as chopped lucerne or sugarcane.

there are some other tricks to ensure your plants are all the same.

Same batch

Much like buying knitting wool from the same dye lot for a uniform look in a knitted garment, buying all your hedge plants from the same supplier at the same time (including a couple of extras) makes it likely that you will have identical plants. Buying more plants later, even from the same supplier, may mean you will have slightly different plants.

Plants from the same batch theoretically should grow to roughly the same height and spread and have similar colouring and growth rates.

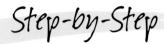

Step-by-Step

HOW TO PLANT A HEDGE

1. Remove any debris from your planting area then improve the soil with added manure or compost. Be generous— use about a bag every metre.

2. Incorporate the manure by digging it in with a fork or spade. If possible, leave it for a week before planting.

3. Place a stake at each end of your proposed hedge. Run a string line between the two stakes.

4. Measure the length between the stakes and then divide it by the number of plants you have, minus one. That is, if you are planting seven plants, then divide the length by six. This figure is the space required between each plant. Mark this length on a stake or other measuring device.

5. Place a plant at each end of the hedge and then set out the other plants in between. Check the distance between each is correct with your measuring stake.

6. Dig a hole for each, remove the plant from the pot and plant.

7. Apply controlled-release fertiliser to each plant, then water well. Allow the water to soak in around the roots.

8. Spread a 5–8 cm layer of mulch around the plants, then water again. Lightly clip the plants. Cut off the tips of all the stems and even-up the height. Maintain with regular pruning.

Same variety

Plants that are named varieties and that are cutting grown, or grafted, are identical as they have been grown from one plant. Buying a named variety ensures uniformity in your hedge.

Even slight changes in soil quality, water, root competition and light along a hedgerow can affect how it grows, so address these issues at planting time. For suggestions on how to do this, see 'Overcoming obstacles' (right).

Ongoing care

Keeping your hedge growing well and forming the screen you want comes down to three main tasks: watering, feeding and pruning.

Watering

Hedges need to be watered regularly, especially when they are first planted. Regular deep watering helps the hedge plants establish a strong, vigorous root system and also allows the plants to get enough water even when they are closely planted. As hedges grow, their dense leafy growth and close spacing can mean they are prone to drying out even when there is rain. To overcome this, install a drip- or micro-irrigation system along the length of your hedge (see 'How to lay an irrigation system', page 102).

OPPOSITE This dwarf box hedge creates a formal edging to display the pansies and breaks up the long space with a geometric pattern.

Overcoming obstacles

There are lots of things in the environment around your hedge that can affect its growth and performance. Sometimes these factors are obvious and sometimes they are difficult to spot. Here are some of the conditions that can have an impact on the growth of your hedge and strategies to overcome or at least manage the issue.

- **Competition:** If part of the hedge is growing near established trees, it will grow more slowly. This growth difference is due to root competition from the nearby trees and may also be due to the effects of shading if the trees block the sun for part of the day.

  Strategy: Use a root barrier and raised beds to separate the hedge from nearby trees. Alternatively, provide the affected plants with extra water and fertiliser.

- **Differences in soil depth:** Soil depth can vary throughout a garden. Sometimes there is underlying rock or the subsoil is closer to the surface in some areas than in others. Plants that are growing in shallow soil may grow more slowly and dry out more quickly. They may be stunted in comparison with plants that have better soil and greater soil depth.

  Strategy: Improve the soil along the row before planting, removing subsurface rocks and digging in gypsum and compost to help improve soil drainage. If necessary, mound up soil prior to planting. Assist plants that are struggling by giving them extra water.

- **Overhead wires:** Plant growth must be kept clear of overhead power lines.

  Strategy: Always look up before you plant a tall hedge. Select a smaller growing variety or move the location of the hedge away from power lines.

- **Underground services:** Avoid planting hedges over underground services such as drains, gas pipes and electrical or telephone conduits.

  Strategy: To find out where underground services such as drains, gas pipes and electrical or telephone conduits are located, consult your house and property plans, or call Dial Before You Dig (1100) a service available throughout Australia and New Zealand that can provide more information about the location of underground hazards. A similar service is available in the US and the UK, and there is also an app for smartphones.

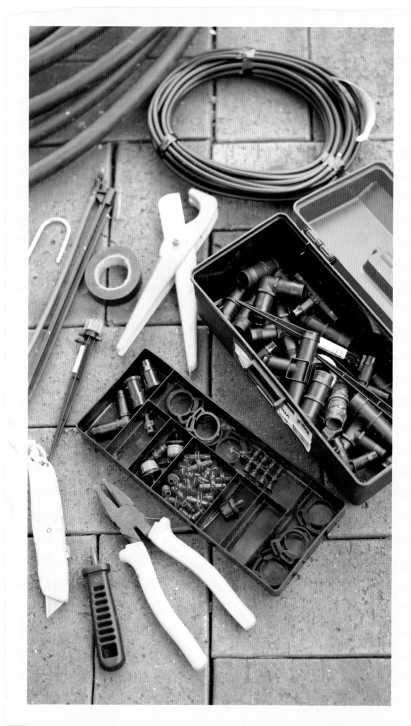

Step-by-Step

HOW TO LAY AN IRRIGATION SYSTEM

Essential tools Pliers, knife or cutting tool to cut pipe, hole-punch, tool box to hold small fittings.

Irrigation fittings Timer, 19 mm polypipe, 13 mm polytube, 4 mm polypipe, micro-spray heads, adjustable drippers, clamps, 13 mm and 19 mm joiners, both in a range of shapes, 4 mm joiners, end stops, goof plugs (to fix mistakes), wire pegs.

1   Install the timer. Some timers have a simple dial that you turn every time you want to water. Simple automatic timers are battery operated; more complex units allow the programming of multiple irrigation lines and must be connected to mains power.

2   Use 19 mm pipe from the tap and around the outer edges of the system. Lay it out on the ground where it is to go.

3   Attach the pipes together with joiners. Secure the pipe to the joiners with a clamp, and tighten with pliers.

4   Use 13 mm polytube to run through the garden. Set it out in rows about 30 cm apart. Attach it to the 19 mm pipe at either end with a joiner and secure with clamps.

5   Make holes in the pipe with the hole-punch where the drippers and spray heads are to be positioned.

6   If you make a hole in the wrong place, push in a goof plug to seal the hole.

7   Attach a 4 mm joiner to the end of the dripper or spray head pipe, if needed, then insert into the pipe.

8   Position the drippers and spray heads. Drippers are good to use on individual plants as they deliver water only to a small area. Spray heads cover a larger area and are best used in the middle of a group of plants, or for watering new seedlings.

9   Turn on the tap to flush out any dirt or debris that's got into the pipes during installation. Once the water is running clear, insert an end stop into the end of every pipe and secure with a clamp.

10 Hold the pipes in place on the ground with wire pegs. If you want to conceal a pipe, cover it with mulch.

> **Tip** To make it easier to push pipes onto the fittings, hold the pipe in hot water for 20–30 seconds, or until softened, then attach.

You can also ensure hedges receive extra water when it rains by encouraging run-off from nearby areas to soak in along the hedge. This can be achieved by cambering hard surfaces such as paths, paving or driveways to direct water towards your hedge.

If the soil under a hedge becomes very dry, and particularly if it appears hydrophobic or water repellent, apply a wetting agent to the soil (either as a mulch or by watering it over the area) to help the soil absorb more water.

Keep the area under the hedge clear of weeds as these compete with the hedge for moisture. Once the area is weeded, cover it with a thin layer of coarse mulch to deter weeds and retain moisture.

Feeding

As a general rule, fertilise hedges at least once a year. Usually, the best time to do this is spring, or at the beginning of its main growth period. Vigorous hedges may need extra fertiliser especially in summer.

If you are frequently trimming your hedge, provide more frequent applications of fertiliser to feed the new growth stimulated by pruning.

The easiest way to apply fertiliser to hedges is with a pelletised fertiliser, which can be readily scattered along the root system. Topping up mulches with compost or well-rotted manure also helps feed hedge plants and nourish the soil.

Pruning

Hedges need regular clipping and training to keep them in shape and at the desired height. Overly tall or wide hedges may also cast shade over lawns or gardens or intrude onto paths or driveways. Hedges should be cut all over—not just at the top—and pruning needs to begin from when the hedge is newly planted.

How to clip a hedge

As pruning is an ongoing chore for the life of the hedge, it is worth investing in the right tools for the job. To prune a hedge you need shears or a hedge trimmer. You also need something to

ABOVE LEFT To ensure that you are making a level cut, use a string line and spirit level.
ABOVE RIGHT Spread a tarpaulin below where you are working to catch the clippings. Rake up the remaining debris.
OPPOSITE Cut just above your string line. If standing on a ladder, move the ladder frequently to prevent accidents caused by over-reaching.

stand on, such as a ladder or platform made of trestles with a solid plank, if your hedge is too high to reach from the ground. Alternatively, invest in a pole pruner with adjustable heads to do the job from ground level.

A drop sheet or tarpaulin is needed to catch the prunings, along with a rake to clean up. To guide your cuts and to keep the top level, use two stakes and a string line. Safety

equipment such as goggles or gloves may also be needed.

Aim to have your hedge slightly wider at the base than the top so that the entire hedge gets even light and has a better chance of receiving moisture when it rains. This approach also stops the hedge becoming top heavy.

To get started, prune across the top of the hedge, cutting it flat and level. To keep your hedge level, set up a string line stretched between two stakes before you start clipping. If you are cutting by 'eye' (that is, without a string line), be sure to stand back frequently to gauge your progress.

Once you are satisfied with the top, prune the sides, starting at the bottom and clipping upwards, cutting so you slightly taper the hedge towards its top.

Finish the task by cutting off any stray branches you've missed and collecting all the prunings. Not only does this tidy the area it also reduces the spread of disease.

How often do you prune?

The frequency of pruning hedges depends on the species of plant you are growing, the type of hedge you are forming and the time of the year.

Most hedges are kept in shape by being pruned once during their growing season, which is often at the end of spring or in early summer when the flush of new growth has hardened up. The later in summer your hedge is pruned the less likely it is you will need to prune it again.

The results from hedge maintenance make the effort required it worthwhile. To maintain a neat, formal look, which is a feature in your garden, you need to prune your hedge two or three times a year, generally between late spring and early autumn. Flowering hedges should be pruned after they've flowered.

If you have fast-growing plants, or are living in a warm climate, your hedge may need even more frequent pruning—often every six weeks between late spring and autumn. If you live in an area with cold or frost during winter, avoid pruning late into autumn as this could encourage soft new growth that may be damaged by frost and look unsightly until it regrows in spring.

Using hedge pruners

The types of tools needed to maintain your hedge depend on the size and extent of your hedge. Use hand shears for short hedges, but if you are maintaining a long hedge invest in an electric, battery or petrol-powered hedge trimmer. Power tools make light work of the job so you don't end up with tired arms. You will still need hand shears for the occasional trim and to snip bits missed by the power tools.

When using an electric trimmer, make sure it's plugged into a safety socket that is fitted with a residual current device or circuit breaker, so the motor cuts out instantly if there's an accident. Keep the electric cable away from the blade at all times—try to have it draped over one shoulder rather than trailing on the ground so you know it isn't near the blade. Finally, always wear appropriate protective equipment, such as goggles and gloves, when using a powered hedge trimmer.

ABOVE Crisp, manicured hedges like these require frequent pruning across their tops and down each side..

From edges to windbreaks

The term hedge can be applied to a row of plants of any height that's being used to form a barrier or edge. A hedge can be a low border that you could step over, up to a row of conifers, more than 30 m tall.

Before you select your hedge plant, particularly in a rural area, make sure the plant is not likely to become a weed. Holly, for example, which is a tough evergreen with spiky leaves, has become weedy in some cold climate areas, while murraya may become invasive in subtropical zones.

Low hedges

Low-growing hedges give your garden style and sophistication. They can be trained to form a pattern (known as a parterre) or grown as a low edge to a path or garden bed.

But, you may ask, what about all that work clipping the damn things? Well here's some good news: there are a host of dwarf, evergreen plants that don't grow much over 1 m tall. Indeed, many stop at 50 cm, the ideal height to edge a garden bed or outline a path or patio. You can even grow them in pots. This makes a low or even dwarf hedge a manageable proposition. They'll still need to be clipped occasionally to keep them in shape, but having one needn't be an enormous amount of work.

Space low hedge plants 30–50 cm apart. Some dwarf selections may be planted even closer, especially if you want to grow a very low hedge for a parterre or garden edging.

Good selections for low hedges are naturally dwarf or very slow-growing varieties including dwarf box (*Buxus microphylla* var. *sempervirens*), coast rosemary (*Westringia fruticosa* 'Jervis Gem'), dwarf lillypillies (*Acmena* and *Syzygium* cultivars such as 'Tiny Trev' and 'Allyns Magic') and dwarf bottlebrush (*Callistemon* 'Great Balls of Fire' and 'Little John'). There are many others to suit every climate zone. See 'Hedge selection' on page 112 for other suggestions.

ABOVE LEFT A low hedge can be spaced very closely together. An easy way to keep the spacings even is to place one plant on the corner of the hedge, then position two more so that all three pots are just touching. Remove the one in the centre. Repeat until all plants are laid out.

ABOVE RIGHT Use shears to cut wayward branches and to keep your hedge neat and tidy.

Tip Keep hand shears sharpened. Blunt blades can damage the plant you are trying to prune and will also make the task much harder.

Dwarf flowering hedges

These low-growing, evergreen selections produce pretty flowers. Prune after flowering to avoid removing flowering wood.

Dwarf escallonia (*Escallonia* 'Pink Pixie')
Dwarf cultivars such as 'Pink Pixie' form a neat, evergreen hedge 30–80 cm high. Escallonia is drought and frost tolerant and a good choice for coastal zones. Grow in full sun. Pink summer flowers. 'Hedge with an Edge' is another dwarf form that's ideal for hedging.

Indian hawthorn (*Rhaphiolepis indica* 'Snow Maiden')
'Snow Maiden' is easily hedged at around 50 cm high. This shrub is drought and frost tolerant and a good coastal choice. Grow in full sun. It has dark-green, leathery leaves and white flowers in spring. There are also pink-flowered varieties.

Tibouchina (*Tibouchina* 'Little Jules')
A small purple-flowered hedge for frost-free climates, 50-90 cm tall. Drought tolerant once established but best with regular watering especially during summer. Flowers are seen in late summer to autumn.

ABOVE Lavender is a fragrent option for a low, informal flowering hedge. Lavender prefers a mild climate and a sunny, well-drained situation.
OPPOSITE A stepped hedge adds interest.

Medium hedges

Hedges of about 1 to 4 m tall are generally used to border a suburban garden, to provide a living fence or a garden divider. With regular pruning, many commonly grown garden shrubs can be trained into medium-sized hedges.

Space plants for a medium hedge 50 cm to 1 m apart depending on the overall size of the plant and how quickly you want the hedge to form. Expect most hedges to take three to five years to give good dense coverage.

Top selections include *Camellia sasanqua*, *Photinia* 'Red Robin', lillypilly (*Acmena smithii* var. *minor*), *Plumbago* 'Royal Cape', bottlebrush (*Callistemon* hybrids) and *Murraya paniculata*.

For other options see 'Hedge selection' on page 112.

Tall hedges

Tall hedges are also referred to as windbreaks. These hedges can be 4 m to 30 m or more tall and are formed by mature evergreen trees. They can be positioned in the environment to provide shelter from prevailing wind and are often a dominant element in the landscape. Tall hedges or windbreaks are widely used in rural areas, particularly to provide shelter from cold wind.

Conifers are the plants that are most widely used to form windbreaks. They are selected because they are tough, dense and evergreen. Other evergreen plants including pittosporum, photinia and holly can be used, as well as native trees and shrubs. It is also possible to use a mixed planting.

Tall hedges can be used to provide corridors through a rural landscape to link areas of native vegetation (for more on this see 'Habitat hedges', page 110). Often a hedge serves several purposes, from providing shelter to improving the environment or even acting as a carbon sink.

If you are planting a hedge as a windbreak for a paddock that contains stock, fence off the hedge area to stop access by stock or other animals. Provide entry to the hedgerow via a gate for ease of watering, mowing and weeding.

Hedges that are planted and protected in this way generally outgrow plants just plonked into the ground, so they repay the extra time and money invested in their establishment.

ABOVE Apples can be espaliered to form an edible hedge.

Useful hedges

As well as dividing up garden or rural spaces or protecting areas from wind, hedges bring other benefits, such as habitat or produce.

Habitat hedges

Habitat hedges provide food and nesting sites for birds and small animals. They also bring insects into the garden. To select a hedge to provide a home or food source for insects, birds and animals choose plants that are dense, evergreen and that produce flowers followed by seeds or fruit. Many Australian native plants are excellent choices for habitat hedges.

Edible hedges

Shrubs, trees and even climbing plants such as passionfruit can be trained as edible hedges or living fences. Hedging is a clever way to incorporate edible plants that require mass planting to produce a worthwhile harvest, such as tea, coffee or blueberries.

Fast hedges

To get a hedge in place quickly there are a number of options. You can, for example, buy advanced plants from a specialist nursery and plant them for an instant hedge.

Another option is to use a fast-growing plant such as clumping bamboo, bananas or giant strelitzia.

Climbers can also be used to create living fences or screens that can substitute for a hedge. Star jasmine (*Trachelospermum jasminoides*), passionfruit (*Passiflora edulis*), wire plant (*Muehlenbeckia complexa*), banksia rose (*Rosa banksiae*), bougainvillea, bower of beauty (*Pandorea jasminoides*) and many other climbers can all be trained on wire or trellis to form a living green wall. All these plants can be pruned and trained to form a dense visual barrier.

The final solution for instant privacy or shelter is to construct a temporary screen such as shadecloth, brushwood fencing or wire while you are waiting for a permanent hedge to establish.

ABOVE Parterres are designed to be viewed from above, so the complex geometric pattern of trained hedging is evident.

Designing with hedges

With hedges there's always the temptation to get a little bit fancy and start shaping plants into balls, domes and other topiary forms. You can use a hedge to add style. Surrounding your vegetable beds with a low hedge turns a vegie patch into a potager.

Parterres

If upper storey windows in your house overlook a flat area of ground, try your hand at a parterre garden, a technique that dates from gardens of the 17th and early 18th centuries.

A parterre or knot garden is created by planting and training low hedges to form a geometric pattern. The beds or spaces formed inside the pattern of hedging can be planted with low-growing plants or filled with gravel.

A spectacular parterre garden has been recreated at Hampton Court Palace at Richmond in London. The 1702 plan for a parterre garden adjacent to the palace was reproduced in a restoration program for the Great Privy garden in 1995. The formal garden was built for William III.

If you are interested in heading down this hedging path, get some books about historic gardens and look for plans of parterre gardens.

Stepped hedges

And don't stop at one hedge—layering hedges of different heights creates a stepped hedge that forms a visually interesting feature. This type of hedge is shown on page 109.

To create a stepped hedge, use plants of different heights with differently shaped and coloured leaves. Plant them in parallel rows for the best effect. For example, a dark green, medium-sized hedge of sasanqua camellia, murraya or lillypilly can form a backdrop to a scented hedge of gardenia or choisya, with a ribbon of dwarf agapanthus or liriope to finish the layered planting scheme.

Hedge selection

These plants are evergreen and can be grown as formal or informal hedges. Many have flowers and are decorative for most of the year.

Plant	Best climate	Size
Abelia (*Abelia* x *grandiflora*)	Cold to subtropical	Medium
Acalypha, copperleaf (*Acalypha wilkesiana*)	Temperate to tropical (frost-free)	Medium
Ardisia, coralberry (*Ardisia* spp.)	All	Small
Aucuba (*Aucuba japonica*)	Cold to temperate	Medium
Azalea (*Rhododendron* hybrids)	Cool to subtropical	Medium
Bamboo (*Bambusa* spp. and other genera)	All (select cold-tolerant species in cold areas)	Medium to tall
Berberis (*Berberis thunbergii*)	Cool to temperate	Small to medium
Bottlebrush (*Callistemon* spp. and cultivars)	Cool to subtropical	Small to tall
Bougainvillea (*Bougainvillea* hybrid cultivars)	Temperate to tropical	Medium to tall
Box (*Buxus* spp.)	Cool to temperate	Small to medium
Camellia (*Camellia japonica, C. sasanqua*)	Cool to subtropical	Small to medium
Conifers (various)	All (select suitable species)	Small to tall
Croton (*Codiaeum* spp.)	Subtopical to tropical	Medium
Diosma (*Coleonema pulchellum*)	Cool to temperate	Small to medium
Duranta (*Duranta erecta*)	Temperate to tropical	Small to medium
Eleagnus, Russian olive (*Elaeagnus angustifolia*)	Cool to subtropical	Small to medium
Escallonia (*Escallonia rubra* and hybrid cultivars)	Cool to temperate	Small to medium
Feijoa, pineapple guava (*Acca sellowiana*)	Cool to sub-tropical	Medium to tall
Fuchsia (*Fuchsia magellanica*)	Cool	Small to medium
Gardenia (*Gardenia augusta*)	Temperate to tropical	Small to medium
Gordonia (*Gordonia axillaris*)	Cool to temperate	Medium
Grevillea (*Grevillea* spp.)	Cool to tropical	Small to medium
Hazel (*Corylus avellana*)	Cool	Medium to tall

Flowers	Comment
White to pink throughout the year	For a small hedge select dwarf cultivars; golden cultivars also available.
Insignificant	Grown for multicoloured foliage.
White flowers followed by long-lasting red berries	Shiny green leaves; good in containers.
Insignificant	Golden variegated forms; good in shade.
Red, pink, purple, mauve, white in spring	Prune after flowering; good in part shade.
Rare	Hedging bamboo (*Bambusa multiplex* 'Alphonse Karr') makes a dense low hedge; blue bamboo (*Drepanostachyum falcatum*) is a good choice for a 3.5 m screen and is cold tolerant. Avoid invasive forms.
Yellow in spring followed by berries	Deciduous and thorny, an ideal barrier plant; many coloured foliage forms available.
Red, pink, mauve or white in spring and autumn	Select named cultivars for even growth; use compact and dwarf varieties for small hedges.
Red, purple, orange, white throughout the year	Bambino series are dwarf selections.
Insignificant	Widely grown evergreen. Japanese box (*Buxus microphylla* var. *japonica*) best choice for temperate zones. Select dwarf cultivars for small hedges.
Red, pink, white from late summer to spring depending on species	Sasanqua camellias tolerate part shade to full sun, japonica camellias best in part shade. Select dwarf varieties for small hedges.
Insignificant	Huge range for dense, evergreen hedges. Avoid fast-growing tall selections in suburban gardens: they require constant pruning and can shade neighbours. Dwarf (*Juniperus* 'Bar Harbor' and others) and fastigiate varieties (*Cupressus* 'Swane's Golden', *Juniperus* 'Skyrocket') suit small gardens.
Insignificant	Grown for vibrantly coloured leaves. Not frost or cold tolerant.
Pink or white in spring	Dwarf and golden foliage varieties available.
Blue, purple or white followed by orange berries	Lime and golden foliage forms; prune after flowering to remove berries, which are weedy.
White in spring followed by black edible fruit	Silver leaves, deciduous, drought / heat hardy. Some species are evergreen.
Red, pink or white in spring	Many named varieties including dwarf forms.
White followed by small edible fruit in summer and autumn	Good seaside tolerance. Protect fruit from fruit fly in affected zones.
Crimson, spring to autumn	Best as an informal hedge, needs little pruning, when flowering attracts birds.
Fragrant white flowers from spring to autumn	Tolerates part shade; 'Radicans' is a dwarf form for low edges, 'Magnifica' is a large, fast-growing variety.
White in autumn and winter	'Silk Screen' is a dense form of hedging.
Red, pink, orange, yellow and white for most of the year	'Orange Marmalade' is a good choice for a tall, dense hedge.
White in spring; nuts in autumn	Deciduous, can be coppiced in winter.

▶

Plant	Best climate	Size
Hebe (*Hebe* x *franciscana*)	Cool to temperate	Small to medium
Hornbeam (*Carpinus betulus*)	Cool	Medium to tall
Hydrangea (*Hydrangea macrophylla*)	Cool to subtropical	Medium
Indian hawthorn (*Rhaphiolepis indica*)	Cool to subtropical	Small to medium
Japanese flowering quince (*Chaenomeles* spp.)	Cool to temperate	Medium
Laurel, Portuguese laurel (*Prunus laurocerasus*)	Cool	Medium
Lavender (*Lavandula angustifolia, L. dentata, L. stoechas* and cultivars)	Cool to temperate	Small
Lillypilly (*Acmena* spp., *Syzygium* spp. and cultivars)	Cool to tropical	Small to tall
Metrosideros, New Zealand Christmas bush (*Metrosideros excelsa*)	Cool to subtropical	Small to tall
Mexican orange blossom (*Choisya ternata*)	Cool	Medium
Michelia, port wine magnolia (*Magnolia figo,* syn. *Michelia figo*)	Temperate to tropical	Medium
Murraya (*Murraya paniculata*)	Temperate to subtropical	Small to medium
Oleander (*Nerium oleander*)	Cool to subtropical	Small to medium
Photinia (*Photinia* x *fraseri, P. glabra* and cultivars)	Cool to temperate	Medium to tall
Pittosporum (*Pittosporum tenuifolium, P. tobira*)	Cool to temperate	Small to medium
Plumbago (*Plumbago auriculata*)	Cool to subtropical	Medium
Rose (*Rosa* spp. and cultivars)	Cool to subtropical	Small to medium
Rosemary (*Rosmarinus officinalis*)	Cool to temperate	Small to medium
Spindletree (*Euonymus japonica*)	Cool to temperate	Medium
Spiraea, may (*Spiraea cantoniensis* and other species)	Cool to sub-tropical	Medium
Viburnum (*Viburnum odoratissimum, V. tinus*)	Cool to subtropical	Medium to tall
Wattle (*Acacia* spp.)	All	Small to tall
Westringia, native rosemary (*Westringia fruticosa*)	Cool to subtropical	Small to medium
Wormwood (*Artemisia* spp.)	Cold to subtropical	Small

Flowers	Comment
Blue, purple or white in spring and autumn with flushes at other times	Variegated forms available. Other species are also suited for hedging, particularly in cooler climate zones.
Insignificant	Deciduous hedge for cold climates.
Blue, purple, pink or white	Deciduous, good in shade. 'Endless Summer' is a long-flowering choice.
White or pink followed by black berries	Compact forms for small hedges; good drought and salt tolerance.
Red, pink, apricot, white in late winter to early spring	Deciduous and thorny, good barrier plant.
White spring flowers followed by black berries	Good drought tolerance; copes with shade and poorly drained soils.
Purple, pink or white winter to summer (depending on species)	Fragrant grey leaves; prune after flowering.
White in spring–summer, followed by red or purple berries	Compact forms for small hedges.
Red brush flowers in summer	Variegated and compact forms available.
White and fragrant in spring and early summer	Golden variegated forms available.
Insignificant but highly fragrant flowers in spring and summer	Shiny evergreen foliage.
White and fragrant, mainly in summer	Select dwarf forms for small hedges, prune to remove berries as species can be weedy in warm climates, flowers best in sun but tolerates shade.
Pink, red, apricot and white flowers from late spring to autumn	Variegated and compact forms available; deciduous; good drought and pollution tolerance; toxic (avoid near stock).
White clusters in spring and summer; black berries	'Everbright', 'Red Robin' and 'Rubens' have repeated flushes of bright red new growth, 'Super Hedge' is fast-growing with bronze new growth.
White flowers (fragrant on *P. tobira*) in spring	Many variegated forms available.
Blue or white flowers throughout the year	'Royal Cape' is not prone to suckering.
Red, pink, orange, yellow or white from spring to autumn; some followed by colourful hips	*Rosa rugosa* forms a dense, salt-tolerant hedge, Rosa 'Softee' is a thornless rose ideal for a low hedge.
Blue or white in spring with flushes throughout the year	Aromatic edible foliage.
White followed by red, spindle-shaped berries in autumn	Lime and golden foliage forms; prune after flowering to remove berries which are weedy.
White or pink in spring	*Spiraea* 'Anthony Waterer' has golden foliage and pink flowers.
White or pink flowers followed by black berries (*V. odoratissimum* flowers are insignificant)	Strong dense growth, *V. tinus* tolerates shade.
Cream to yellow; different species flower at different times of the year	Good choice for habitat hedge, windbreak, fast screen. Some wattles are short-lived. *Acacia* 'Limelight' forms a dense low hedge with lime green foliage. *A. baileyana* and *A. howittii* form good medium to tall hedges. *A. decurrens* is an excellent windbreak planting for cooler climates.
White or mauve throughout the year	Compact forms for small hedges; good drought and salt tolerance.
White or yellow daisies	Grown for silver foliage.

CHAPTER 8

Planting in containers

Why do I need to read this chapter?

- For information on growing mediums for pots.

- For tips on potting, re-potting and caring for containerised plants.

- For suggestions on what plants are appropriate for containers.

Putting into pots

Lots of gardeners grow plants in pots, but where there's no access to soil, such as in an apartment or small house, container growing is the only option for a would-be gardener.

In other situations, containers are used to customise or control the growing conditions for plants. Containers allow gardeners to grow plants that are unsuited to the local soil conditions—such as camellias grown in acidic potting mix in alkaline areas—or where there's just not enough space or permanency for in-ground growing.

Container gardening is a good option for people with disabilities or those who are on the move and want to take their garden with them. Potted plants are also used for indoor and outdoor decoration.

Potting mix

Potting mix (also known as potting compost) has been developed for use as the growing medium in pots. Unlike soil, which can set like concrete, fail to drain or even produce weeds when it is added to a pot, potting mixes are free draining, sterile and compatible with plants. A well-composted mix has the right balance of particle sizes to hold air and water and has some nutrients to feed the plants that are grown in it.

Bagged potting mixes were first produced for gardeners in the 1960s. These early mixes were formulated in the UK and are still known as John Innes mixes. They were formulated by mixing loam and peat moss.

Potting mix standards

In Australia, potting mixes are made from composted pine bark. They were developed as an offshoot to the timber industry. Today they are assisting in recycling wood and green wastes. Australia has led the world in the development of soil-less potting mixes, and its soil scientists have developed quality standards for bagged products.

The development of good quality Australian mixes, including a national standard for potting mixes, is down to the good work of Adelaide-based CSIRO scientist Kevin Handreck, who developed standards for potting mixes. The standard falls under the control of Standards Australia and receive the same scrutiny as any building or manufacturing standard in Australia. They are indicated on bagged potting mixes by a series of ticks in a logo on the bag.

BELOW Potted plants can be used as stylish decorating pieces that are also portable.

ABOVE LEFT Bagged potting mixes must conform to a Standard to ensure they are suited to plant growth.
ABOVE RIGHT Mulch on the surface of pots keeps the mix cool and prevents soil washing out during watering.

The Standard for Potting Mix specifies quality checks for potting mix manufacturers and recommends two levels: Regular and Premium. Premium has added fertiliser to sustain growth.

When buying a potted mix that meets the Standard for Potting Mix gardeners can be reasonably sure that it will provide suitable growing conditions for a wide range of plants.

Specialised mixes can be found for a range of plants including Australian native plants, acid-loving plants, orchids, cactus and succulents, African violets, vegetables, camellias and azaleas, and roses. There are also seed-raising and propagating mixes. These provide the growing conditions best suited to seedlings and cuttings.

Safety precautions

Take care opening bags of potting mix as, like all soils, composts and mulch it may contain *Legionella* organisms. *Legionella longbeachae* is a naturally occurring bacterium found in the natural environment—including in compost and soil. It was first isolated in Long Beach, California in the USA.

Occasionally this strain of bacteria can build up into large and dangerous levels in bags of potting mix, so care must be taken when opening bags of potting mix and when handling potting mixes. Warnings are now posted on bags of potting mixes and should be read and followed to minimise any chance of infection.

It's important to avoid breathing in dust while opening bags of potting mix. Wear a mask if you are unwell or have a compromised immune system and, if necessary, when moistening the mix with water. Also take care watering pot plants as strong jets of water can disturb bacteria. As a further precaution, always wash your hands after handling potting mix—or indeed any form of compost or garden soil. Finally, avoid eating while gardening.

ABOVE Make your own potting mix by combining composts, sand and bark.

Potting mix combinations

Test the combinations below, adjusting the proportions to suit your particular needs. It's a good idea to grow a test batch of plants and check drainage and pH to ensure your mix is suited to plant growth.

Use	Ingredients	Method
Seed or propagating mix	Perlite and coir peat	Combine in equal parts
General free-draining mix	Mushroom compost, composted pine bark, coarse sand	Combine in equal parts
Cactus and succulent mix	Mushroom compost, coarse sand, pine bark, coir peat, perlite	Combine in equal parts
Orchid mix	coarse bark	Add coarse sand or coir peat as required

Make your own potting mix

Although there are a large number of commercial potting mixes available, many gardeners are keen to make their own. This is usually to tailor a potting mix to a specialist plant collection, to save money where large numbers of potted plants are being managed, or to use up waste material.

Potting mixes can also be amended with the addition of extra compost, sand or even garden loam. This is done where plants are being grown permanently in large containers, as the added material tends to hold nutrients and also doesn't decompose,

thus reducing the likelihood of the potting mix slumping in the container over time. Slumping is where the volume of the mix gradually breaks down, reducing the amount of potting mix in the container.

For hanging baskets, try adding light-weight materials, such as vermiculite or perlite, to your potting mix to reduce its weight, making it easier, and safer, to hang.

If you are making your own mix, or amending a commercial bagged mix, take care not to introduce pests, diseases or weeds. Commonly available ingredients that can be used to make potting mixes include bark compost; homemade or mushroom compost; rice hulls; washed river or coarse sand; peat including coir peat; perlite;

vermiculite; and aged manure. Select and combine those materials that can provide the properties you need in your mix such as drainage, nutrition, bulk and water retention.

For extra water-holding capacity, add water crystals following the manufacturer's recommendations. Slow-release or pelletised fertiliser can also be incorporated.

 Tip When you are making up a batch of your own potting mix, use a spade and wheelbarrow or even a concrete mixer to thoroughly mix the ingredients together.

How to re-pot a plant

Re-potting is a simple but neglected task. All you are doing is taking a plant out of one pot and putting it into another. This is done to move a plant into a larger pot with more growing area or to provide fresh potting mix.

As plants outgrow their containers they need to be re-potted. It is best to move a plant into a slightly larger container (2–3 cm larger all round), but in some instances the plant can be root-pruned and returned to its original pot with fresh potting mix.

Moving a plant into a much larger container than its root ball needs can retard growth. It may lead to the plant failing to thrive or even to plant death if the plant is sitting in a large expanse of mix where it may not be watered correctly. Weeds may colonise the extra soil not being used by the plant. It is also a waste of resources and money to use pots that are too big, as large pots hold considerably more potting mix than smaller pots. If you want to use a large pot and don't have an appropriately sized plant, put several plants in the one pot.

If you have a lot of potted plants, it makes sense to re-pot several pots at the same time. It is efficient and a good use of resources. This approach

LEFT Put large or heavy pots into position before adding the potting mix.

ABOVE Pots of a similar shape, size or colour create a uniform and pleasing texture in a garden.

Re-potting checklist

- ✓ Soak the root ball thoroughly so it is wet before re-potting.
- ✓ Check for pests and diseases. Treat if necessary.
- ✓ Remove weeds, including their roots or bulbs.
- ✓ Prune damaged roots.
- ✓ Don't plant the plant deeper in the pot than it was in its old pot.

can also mean savings on potting mixes if you can bulk buy. To do the job as efficiently as possible, have all the materials you need to hand.

The materials needed to re-pot include new or clean pots, potting mix, water, a drop sheet to catch the mess, trowel, secateurs, wetting agents and a container to hold discarded mix. A piece of shadecloth or fly wire to cover the drainage hole or holes in the base of the pot is optional. This is done

to stop potting mix leaking out from the pot through the drainage hole and prevents insects getting in.

If you are re-potting or potting up a number of plants, estimate how much potting mix is needed to fill all the pots. It may be cheaper or more efficient to order a bulk delivery of potting mix from a landscape supplier, or if you are buying a number of bags of potting mix at once, you may be able to get a discount when you buy.

Step-by-Step

HOW TO RE-POT A PLANT

If the pot is large, put it into its final position before it is filled up with potting mix and plants.

1 When the roots of a plant are coming out the drainage holes, it's time to re-pot it. If you're re-using the pot, remove all potting mix, clean and sterilise with a disinfectant such as diluted bleach, Dettol or tea-tree oil. If desired, cover the drainage holes in the base of the pot with a piece of flywire.

2 Partially fill the new pot with potting mix. Use only enough mix to support the root ball so the top of the root ball is near the top of the new pot. Don't bury the roots more deeply in the new pot than they were originally.

3 Take the plant out of its existing pot, cutting or breaking the pot if necessary to avoid damage to the plant or its root system.

4 Trim away roots that have grown through the drainage holes in the base as well as any spiralling roots. If the plant is going back into the same pot, trim off a thin layer of roots from the outside of the root ball.

5 Position the plant in its new pot, placing it so it is centred in the pot. If you are planting a bare-rooted plant in a pot, mound the soil in the base of the pot to form a platform that supports the roots.

6 Fill in around the root ball with fresh potting mix. Water as you go to avoid air bubbles or large gaps in the mix. Firm the plant into position. Top with mulch. Add slow-release fertiliser to the top of your pot, unless it is included in the potting mix.

Tip If the plant is difficult to get out of the pot try soaking it first in a large container of water. If you are moving a plant from garden soil into a pot, gently hose off the soil before placing it in the pot.

Caring for pots

Plants that are growing in containers need regular care and attention. They need watering, fertilising, pruning, pest and disease control, weeding and re-potting. Potted plants also need more attention in hot or cold weather than the same plant growing in the ground, as they are more likely to suffer from temperature extremes.

Watering and drainage

Most containerised plants need more frequent watering than the same plant growing nearby in the ground. To know when to water a potted plant, look at the plant and feel the soil. If the plant appears wilted or the soil feels dry, the plant will need watering. Don't allow plants to dry out, as potting mix can be difficult to re-wet. If plants do dry out and water fails to soak in, apply a soil-wetting agent or dunk the entire pot in a bucket of water to rehydrate the soil. Also, don't allow water to sit in saucers under potted plants—empty them often. Regularly check that water is draining through drainage holes in the base of pots. These holes are vital to the health of the plant and can be blocked by roots. Having pots elevated on pot feet or chocks allows for drainage holes to be easily monitored.

OPPOSITE Small edible plants, such as these chillies, create an ornamental as well as productive display for a sunny situation.

Fertilising

Apply small amounts of fertiliser throughout the growing period. This can take the form of a granulated specialist fertiliser such as a citrus food for a potted citrus or azalea food for a potted azalea, a pelletised slow-release formulation or regular liquid feeds. Be guided by recommended application rates from manufacturers.

Pruning

Many potted plants benefit from regular tip pruning to maintain a compact shape. Unless the plant is grown for fruit, prune after flowering. Regularly groom potted plants to remove dead leaves and spent flowers.

Pest and disease control

Check potted plants regularly for signs of pests or diseases, even if the plants are growing in an isolated environment, such as a high-rise balcony or rooftop garden. If the plant is growing indoors and requires spraying or other chemical treatment, take it outdoors to a sheltered spot before spraying.

Weeding

Hand weed any weeds that appear immediately. Remove any weed roots or corms when re-potting. Apply mulch to the surface to reduce weeds.

Re-potting

Re-pot most potted plants every two to five years, depending on how actively they grow. Watch for signs of water stress, nutrient deficiencies and roots protruding from drainage holes. An unstable pot is another indication that re-potting is needed. To avoid total re-potting, remove cores of potting mix from time to time and replace with fresh potting mix or compost or apply compost to the surface as a mulch.

Protecting potted plants from damage

Exposure to climate and weather extremes can spell disaster for potted plants. Temperatures inside pots can be colder than the surrounding temperatures on cold days and hotter than air temperature on hot days. Plants in pots are more likely to die or suffer root damage in very cold or hot conditions than the same plant growing nearby in the garden with its roots in soil. Some pots can crack in very cold or frosty conditions.

Plants in pots are also more likely to be blown over in strong winds than garden plants and dry out faster in hot or windy conditions than plants growing in the soil.

To protect plants from damage use some of the following strategies.

- Group pots together so they shade each other.
- Place plastic pots into ceramic pots.
- Wrap pots in insulating material such as cardboard, bubble wrap or straw.
- Move pots to sheltered positions to avoid extreme heat or cold.

Special containers

Pots come in all shapes and sizes and plants can be grown in containers in extreme situations. Here are some tips on caring for those special containers.

Hanging baskets

The main concern with hanging baskets is that they are prone to drying out. This can occur rapidly on hot or windy days. To reduce moisture stress, line fibre baskets with perforated plastic, add water-holding crystals to the potting mix, or grow plants in large plastic hanging baskets. Remember, temperatures inside plastic hanging baskets can become extremely hot on warm days, which can kill plant roots. On hot or windy days take the basket down and position where it is cool and sheltered to reduce stress.

Vertical gardens

These gardens make good use of vertical spaces to help green urban and city environments. Vertical garden systems are available that include a watering system, growing medium and framework to support the garden. Take the weight of the system along with access to water into account when positioning a vertical garden. Plants that grow well in a minimal amount of soil do best in these gardens. Choices for success include bromeliads and epiphytes. Water is usually supplied via a watering system installed in the garden. Check it often for blockages.

Step-by-Step

HOW TO PLANT A HANGING BASKET

1 Half fill a hanging basket with potting mix.

2 Arrange the plants in the basket. Remove or add potting mix so the top level of the root ball is just below the top rim of the basket.

3 Backfill around the plants with potting mix, making sure that it is pushed into all the gaps between each plant.

4 Water well, and attach the hooks and chains.

 Tip Don't mount hanging baskets so high they can't be easily watered or they will risk being forgotten.

OPPOSITE This vertical garden is mainly planted with succulents to form a living picture.

ABOVE Groups of containers or raised garden beds provide growing space in areas without access to soil. To contain run-off, ensure there's drainage, and, if the area is on a roof, a waterproof membrane in place.

Balcony gardens

Balcony gardens usually receive light from one direction, meaning they can be very shaded for most of the day but are exposed for a part of the day to very hot sun. Avoid the temptation to only have small pots on balconies— a grouping of several large pots not only looks better and provides better growing conditions, it also allows you to experiment with a range of plants and plant combinations. When choosing plants, consider the amount of light and wind the balcony receives. Overhanging floors cast deep shadow even on a balcony with a sunny aspect, so this must be considered. To make large pots easier to move around, sit them on low platforms with wheels.

Roof gardens

Roof gardens have their own unique problems. The weight of containers and constraints of moisture run-off are the main issues to be confronted when growing a roof garden. Like plants in hanging baskets, roof gardens can also be exposed to extremes, particularly heat and drying from wind. Before placing containers on a roof space, examine where the run-off drains. Ideally roof gardens are built on top of a waterproof membrane with drainage to take water off the roof area. Before adding any large structures such as built-in planter boxes, pergolas, paving and furniture, check with an engineer about the potential weight involved. For safety, don't position pots where they can be blown off the roof or tipped over an edge. Have water available and good access to pots and soil when it is time to re-pot. For success, concentrate on growing tough, drought hardy plants that are wind resistant.

ABOVE Arranging pots at different heights adds impact to the display.

Indoor plants

Lack of light and extremes of temperature are two factors that can adversely affect indoor plants. Provide indoor plants with as much natural light as possible. Also take care to keep them out of draughts and away from the direct impact of air-conditioners or heaters. Indoor plants benefit from a spell outdoors in a shaded or semi-shaded situation such as under a tree or in a shadehouse. Use this period outdoors to feed your plant and treat it if necessary for pests or diseases. When taking plants indoors, always check the pot for unwanted guests such as snails, slugs or even spiders that may be under the rim of the pot. Re-pot indoor plants regularly to keep them in good health.

Step-by-Step

HOW TO PLANT BULBS IN POTS

1 Put together a selection of bulbs—choose ones that are different heights and flower at different times. Half fill a pot with potting mix.

2 Remember that bulbs should be planted at a depth equal to twice the width of the bulb. So place the largest bulbs, such as daffodils, at the bottom and then cover with potting mix.

3 Plant the next smallest bulbs, and continue forming layers of bulbs until all have been planted.

4 Water well. Place in a sunny spot and keep moist. When the bulbs start coming into flower, move the pot into full view or bring inside as a beautiful temporary display.

Epiphytes on boards

Epiphytic plants such as some ferns, orchids and bromeliads can be grown without soil. These plants can be grown in mulch under trees, attached to logs or trunks, on rocks or mounted on backing boards and then attached to a wall or tree trunk. They require regular moisture and filtered light. Apply a liquid plant food from time to time.

Mulches for pots

Not many people use mulch in pots but there are lots of good reasons to top off a pot with a layer of mulch. It can be an organic material, such as compost, pine bark or sugar cane; or an inorganic mulch of gravel, pebbles, decomposed sandstone or granite.

Mulch performs the same role in pots as it does for garden soils. It helps maintain moisture, deter weed growth, keep potting mix cool and, with organic mulches, provide some slow-release fertiliser as the mulch decomposes. Mulches also reduce the chance of potting mix being washed from the top of pots while they are being watered. When dry-loving plants such as cactus and succulents are grown in pots, a layer of inorganic mulch over the surface of the potting mix can also keep the plant in better health.

Where a potted plant is standing in a cover pot, mulch can be used to conceal the inner pot. Sphagnum moss is very useful for this purpose. As with mulch on the surface of garden soils, don't apply it so thickly as to prevent water from penetrating the potting mix below the mulch. A 2–3 cm layer of mulch is all that's required.

RIGHT Pebble mulch is both decorative and practical. It prevents weed growth and the potting mix washing away during watering.
OPPOSITE A mix of upright and trailing plants in a pot planted with contrasting flowers and foliage is eye-catching.

Troubleshooting

Plants grown in containers suffer the same pests, diseases and problems that beset garden plants, but also have their own innate problems.

Drying out

It is vital to keep potted plants well watered. Don't rely on rainfall as it often fails to reach potted plants, especially those under eaves or shelter.

If a plant is not watered and dries out, the potting mix may shrink from the side of the pot. This means that when water is applied, instead of soaking into the mix and reaching the roots, it flows down the inside of the pot. The best solution to this problem is to dunk the pot and its contents in a large container of water to re-wet the potting mix. If this is not possible, water over the potting mix with a soil wetting agent.

Step-by-Step

HOW TO PLANT A TERRARIUM

Generally, any plant that can grow in low light can be planted in a terrarium. By using a terrarium you can control humidity and warmth, thus providing a stable environment for delicate plants such as ferns, orchids, African violets and carnivorous plants.

1 Select a container. Any glass vessel can be used, with or without a lid.

2 Line the base of the container with coarse gravel and a 2 cm-layer of charcoal, to absorb any wastes or sour odours.

3 To stop the potting mix from combining with the charcoal, place a thin layer of paper towel, coir fibre, shredded bark or sphagnum moss over the charcoal layer.

4 Add some potting mix then arrange the plants in place, and plant.

5 Mulch with coloured pebbles or sphagnum moss. Mist or water lightly. Replace the lid, if you're using one.

6 Every week, check if the potting mix has dried out and water or mist if needed. Once a month, spray with weak foliar fertiliser.

Hot pots

On warm sunny days pots can heat up. Temperatures in pots can be much higher than the surrounding air temperature. Temperatures above 35°C inside a pot can damage roots. On a hot summer day, temperatures inside pots can easily reach 40°C or even higher, which causes root damage and even plant death. As a general rule, plastic pots allow potting mixture to get hot whereas glazed ceramic pots maintain potting mix at a more even temperature. Other options to keep pots cool are to shade pots on hot days, place plastic pots inside larger ceramic ones, group pots together or just move them to a shadier spot while it is hot.

Wet conditions

Many of us like to stand our pots in saucers to stop mess leaking from the pot to the surface below. This is often very important on balconies of apartments where there's a risk of water dripping down onto the people living below. However, if pots are left standing in water the potting mix can become waterlogged and plant roots may rot. Water in plant saucers is okay on very hot days or with water-loving plants, but generally speaking it is not healthy for the plants. Added to this, it can also be a breeding ground for mozzies.

One option is to raise your pots on pot feet and position saucers underneath. They can be easily lifted out and emptied once the pot has stopped draining.

LEFT Pots that are slightly elevated on pot feet drain better than those on the ground. Pot feet also make it easier to check for wayward roots growing through the drainage holes.

Ants

Ants can also cause problems in potted plants by creating large air-filled chambers in and around plant roots. You are more likely to encounter ants in pots with very dry mix. One way to keep pots free of ants is to elevate the pots on pot feet and stand the pot feet in water (like the old meat safe). The water around the pot feet deters ants. If you suspect there are ants in potting mix soak the entire pot in water. If this doesn't flush them out, re-pot.

Curl grubs

Curl grubs are very damaging in pots. If you have a potted plant that is failing to thrive or is wilting when the potting mix is not dry, it may have been infested with these small, white, C-shaped insects. They are beetle larvae from various beetles including African lawn beetles and cockchafers. The beetles lay eggs in potting mix and, when they hatch, they feed on plant roots until they pupate and emerge as beetles. Plants can die if the curl grubs damage the roots. The quickest way to deal with curl grubs is to re-pot the plant, removing the curl grubs from the potting mix and disposing of them by squashing or feeding to chooks or birds. There are also chemicals available to control curl grubs in potting mix.

Earthworms

Earthworms are great in the soil but in pots they can cause problems by burrowing through the potting mix and leaving air pockets. When roots hit air pockets they die back. Earthworms can also indicate poorly drained potting mix. They may have been present in the pot when you re-potted or have entered via the drainage hole. Elevate the pot, allow the soil to become drier (cut back on watering), remove organic mulch or repot into fresh potting mix to remove earthworms.

RIGHT In areas that experience very cold winter conditions, plants can be damaged and pots may crack. Bubble wrap will insulate the pots against the cold.

Cold damage

Potted plants are also more at risk of damage from cold than the same plants growing nearby in the soil. This is because temperatures are colder in pots in winter than in the soil, which has more insulation. Cold can kill plants outright or damage their root systems. Freezing conditions can cause susceptible pots to split. Protect cold-sensitive plants through winter by moving pots into warmer positions such as inside a glasshouse, plastic-covered igloo, or conservatory, or onto a sheltered patio. If this is not possible, try clustering pots together, standing pots in cover pots or wrapping pots in plastic (bubble wrap is ideal) or straw. This last measure must be taken in areas with extremely cold winters especially if pots are not frost safe.

Selecting plants for containers

Just about any plant can be grown in a pot for a short time, and this is the usual means of growing plants for sale in nurseries. Most plants do best if they are transferred from their nursery pot into the garden.

However, some plants will grow better than others in pots in the long-term. As a general guide, a plant will do well in a pot long-term if it is naturally small growing with a small, shallow or compact root ball. Plants with low nutrient needs are also better adapted to container growing than fast-growing, vigorous plants. Plants to avoid growing in containers include most climbers, trees, large shrubs such as hibiscus and roses, and root vegetables such as carrots or parsnip.

Just about any plant can be grown in a pot if it is grown as a bonsai specimen. Bonsai is a method of training plants so they stay permanently small, while developing interesting shapes and forms. Plants are kept unnaturally small through confinement to shallow pots and containers and regularly pruning their roots, thus restricting their growth.

TOP Succulents often grow well in containers and work well as table decorations.
ABOVE Bonsai is a centuries-old growing technique that keeps plants small for containers.

Perfect plants for pots

The following selection of plants grow well in pots. Make sure they are planted in appropriately sized containers and given the correct amount of sun or shade.

Annuals (especially pansy, viola, petunia, impatiens, lobelia)

Aspidistra

Azaleas (evergreen, especially small-growing varieties)

Bamboo (dwarf or clumping bamboos)

Bamboo palm *(Chamaedorea seifrizii)*

Bougainvillea (miniature forms only including 'Raspberry Ice' and Bambino Series)

Bromeliads

Bulbs (miniature spring-flowering bulbs such as daffodils, grape hyacinth, blue star flower)

Cactus

Camellia (particularly small *Camellia sasanqua* varieties and hybrids including 'Marge Miller', 'Setsugekka')

Clivia

Cumquat

Cymbidium orchid

Eucharist lily *(Eucharis amazonica)*

Ferns

Fuchsia (particularly basket varieties such as 'Swingtime')

Gardenia

Happy plants *(Dracaena fragrans, D. marginata)*

Herbs

Hydrangeas (miniature varieties, 'Endless Summer' varieties)

Indian hawthorn *(Rhaphiolepis indica)*

Japanese maples (dwarf and weeping forms including *Acer palmatum* 'Atropurpureum')

Lemons (dwarf varieties 'Lots a' Lemons', 'Meyer')

Lillypilly (particularly clipped or dwarf forms including *Syzygium* 'Elite', 'Beach Ball')

Looking glass plant *(Coprosma repens)*

Mother-in-law's tongue *(Sansevieria trifasciata)*

Rhapis palms *(Rhapis excelsa, R. humilis)*

Succulents (including *Agave attenuata*, crassula, kalanchoe, sedum, sempervivum)

CHAPTER 9

After-planting care and maintenance

Why do I need to read this chapter?

- To learn how to care for plants after they go in the ground.

- To find out what maintenance is needed for transplants.

- For information about long-term care for established plants.

Looking after plants

How you care for a plant once it has gone in the ground determines how well it grows and performs. A few weeks of intensive care after planting may be enough to see a plant well established and on its way to becoming a valuable asset to the garden. Plants that are neglected after planting may die— usually due to lack of water—or be damaged in a way that impedes their growth and development.

The size of the plant, its root system, the nature of the soil, the amount of soil moisture and the weather all play a part in how well a plant survives in the ground. Protecting the plant from pests—including browsing animals— can also help it to survive.

The amount of care a plant needs after planting is dependent upon how well suited it is to its growing environment and the nature of its growth. The amount of care that will be required should be a factor that's taken into account when planting occurs. Plants that have a high need for ongoing maintenance should be easily accessible.

The way a plant is grown may also determine its need for ongoing care and maintenance. For example, a fast-growing plant grown as a hedge may require regular pruning, watering and feeding while the same plant grown in a shrub border may need very little attention at all.

To maintain plants in good health and vigour they need regular watering and feeding. Most also require mulches to be renewed, weeds to be removed and pruning to be carried out.

In wind-exposed areas, new plantings also do better if they are protected from strong winds with a temporary windbreak. Some also require staking.

In addition plants should be checked from time to time for signs of pests or diseases and to ensure that they are growing strongly without interference from surrounding plants.

Watering after planting

Don't plant and forget! To understand why it is not a good idea to just plant and forget it helps to understand how the plant was functioning in its pot prior to planting out.

Plants in pots in a nursery are watered once if not more frequently each day. They are growing in potting mix, which is well drained. When a plant is taken out of its pot and placed into a hole in the ground it takes time for the root system to extend into the new soil. While the plant remains reliant on its small root system that's still encased in potting mix it is highly dependant on regular water. If the potting mix dries out the roots shrink back, making the mix difficult to re-wet even if the surrounding soil is moist.

Care for a recently planted plant is not just giving it regular water but watering the area where the roots are. In all but extreme drought or heat wave situations, watering can be reduced once the roots enter the surrounding soil and are able to gain access to the surrounding soil moisture.

Certain cultivation techniques can help plants survive with less regular watering after planting. Creating a shallow saucer or crater around the plant is one way of helping a plant survive. This shape captures water and allows it to soak slowly into the soil and into the potting mix. A thin layer of coarse mulch over the shallow crater keeps the roots cool but allows the rain and other water from hosing or irrigation to still reach the soil.

A low, raised mound around the plant can also act as a moat, holding water that's applied to the roots so that it can't drain away. Until they have sent roots into the surrounding soil, new plantings will need more water than established plants nearby.

LEFT Making a depression or forming a low mound at planting will help funnel or contain the water so it is better able to reach the plant's roots.
OPPOSITE Newly transplanted plants should be protected from extreme elements to maintain strong and healthy growth. This protection can be removed when the plant is established.

DIY water systems

If you are planting a new plant and know you won't be able to return regularly to water and care for it, there are certain measures you can take to assist its survival.

Provide water

This can be done by installing a watering system or by placing a container of water that can drip feed the plant. The simplest method is an upended flask of water that slowly soaks into the soil. There are also many commercial systems available designed to drip feed water to plants in the days or weeks after planting.

Increase soil water

Water crystals and blocks placed in the soil around the root system can provide water for the developing roots. When the plant is watered, polycarbonate crystals reabsorb water. Using these types of materials will increase the cost of planting, but it does also increase the plant's chance of survival. Incorporating too many crystals into the soil can have adverse effects on the plant, so follow the recommended rate on the container. It's a good idea to hydrate the crystals first and then mix them into the planting soil.

Water to the roots

Another method is to insert a tube such as a short length of irrigation pipe next to a plant so that the water is delivered directly to the root system. This type of system works well when new plantings are being watered from a tank or water truck.

ABOVE LEFT An upended bottle with a dripping nozzle allows for less frequent watering in hard to access areas. **ABOVE RIGHT** Polycarbonate crystals soaked in water prior to adding to the soil will help plants survive longer between watering. **OPPOSITE** A watering can is a quick way to give a new plant much-needed watering.

Mulch for healthy growth

Mulch is spread around a plant at planting time. As part of any ongoing maintenance and care, you should check that the mulch is allowing moisture through to the soil below. This can be done after watering or after rain, by scraping aside the mulch and feeling the soil below the surface.

If the soil is dry despite watering, remove some of the mulch if it has been applied too thickly, or gently open up the mulch if it has formed a mat or water-repellent surface. Use a fork to open up or remove excess mulch.

Also check that the mulch hasn't built up around the stem of a plant. If it has, simply brush or scrape it away.

Although mulch is used to inhibit weed growth, weeds can germinate in mulch or even grow up through mulch from the soil below. As part of ongoing maintenance, hand weed or spot treat with herbicide any weeds that are growing in or through the mulch.

After a while organic mulch breaks down, so from time to time top up mulches with fresh material. It is generally not necessary to remove the old mulch.

In areas where termites are active also regularly check wood-based mulches for signs of termite activity such as mudding and live termites in mud-encased tunnels. To avoid termites in mulch, use inorganic mulch such as gravel, stones or sand.

ABOVE Check that soil below mulch is moist. Apply mulch loosely around the plant so moisture can still reach the soil below.

OPPOSITE Mulch spread around plants deters weeds and insulates the soil against the heat. This mulch of sugar cane has been spread over a natural leaf litter mulch.

Fertiliser and nutrient needs

As most garden plants grow, they benefit from the application of extra nutrients. This can be given as a liquid and watered over the plant; slow-release prills or pellets can be scattered around the plant; or powdered fertiliser can be dug into the soil or between the rows. If you are digging fertiliser into the soil take care not to damage plant roots.

However, not all plants need extra fertiliser after planting. If the plant is growing in a soil that's been enriched with slow-release fertilisers or organic matter before planting, or where the plant is not receiving additional water, it is unnecessary—and may even be damaging—to apply extra fertiliser unless the plant is actively growing and showing signs of deficiency.

Fertilising a plant encourages new growth, which in turn demands extra water and care. If the plant's need for additional water is not met the new growth may die, so hold off on more nutrients if possible.

Plants that have been forced into growth by the over-application of fertiliser may also develop soft, sappy growth, which may be highly attractive to insects or susceptible to diseases, leaving the plant open to attack.

RIGHT Only apply fertiliser when the previous fertiliser has been expended and the plant is actively growing.

Plant protection from animals

New plantings are often at risk of damage from insects or browsing animals. If you are planting in an area where there are wild or feral browsing animals (such as rabbit, wallaby, deer, possum or birds such as brush turkeys or blackbirds) or grazing animals such as sheep, cattle or goats, it is necessary to put a barrier around the plant to stop it being eaten. This can be fencing around an entire area or a hoarding or barrier around individual plants.

Free-ranging poultry can also damage new plants and should be excluded from new plantings using fencing or wire. Other pets including cats, dogs and rabbits may also interfere with new plantings.

Hessian or plastic sleeves slipped over stakes around a new plant are often all that's needed to provide protection for the plant. These types of covers can also reduce water loss and protect new plants from cold, frost or wind damage.

Where cats are a problem, surround new plantings with wire, or deter them by using wire or plastic matting over the soil. There are spiked plastic mats available that can be laid around new plantings to deter cats.

If you have some form of protection around a new planting, check that it is well attached but that water is still able to reach the plant. Remove weed growth from within the barrier and check for any insect activity.

Smaller pests can also damage new plants. Where snails and slugs are active, use a snail bait or a barrier to protect plants. Seedlings are particularly vulnerable to snail or slug attacks. Commercial baits, caffeine sprays, beer traps and barriers such as grit, sawdust or crushed eggshell which are laid in a

ABOVE LEFT Plastic beakers, cut down PET or other waxed containers, can be pressed into the soil to deter snails and slugs.
ABOVE CENTRE Three small stakes and a length of mesh or shadecloth can be used to protect new plants from browsing animals such as rabbits.
ABOVE RIGHT A sturdy plastic sleeve supported by three cane stakes protects plants from animals and provides a buffer against the wind and the cold.

ring around vulnerable plants can all be used for protection from snails.

Pests within the soil can attack new plantings. Cutworms in particular are insects that live in soil and can damage newly planted vegetables and annuals. To protect plants, make a sleeve from a takeaway cup or glass, or a tin with top and bottom removed, and slip it over the plant, pushing it down into the soil. Once the plant has begun to grow, the barrier can be removed.

What about staking?

Tall or grafted plants, and plants growing in wind-exposed situations, often benefit from being staked at planting. A stake is simply a straight piece of timber or metal that acts as an anchor to support the stem of a plant. It can be a single upright stake inserted beside the plant or two or even three stakes placed around the plant.

One stake is generally used to support a standard or grafted standard plant or herbaceous plant such as a dahlia or chrysanthemum, or a vegetable plant such as a tomato, which may be broken by wind or rain or the sheer weight of its blooms or fruit. This stake is usually permanent and is needed for the life span of the plant.

Two or three stakes are used to provide support for a tree or transplant where staking is only needed on a temporary basis until the tree or shrub has developed a strong root system that is able to support the plant.

However, not all plants need to be staked. Unstaked plants tend to develop stronger stems and roots than staked plants, making them less susceptible to damage in the longer term.

To protect the trunk of the tree from damage from the tie, it is best to use some type of soft tie including budding tape, a commercial plant tie or a length of pantyhose. To further reduce damage the plant tie can be arranged in a figure of eight pattern.

Step-by-Step

HOW TO STAKE

1 Using a mallet, drive in a stake either side of the plant.

2 Place a soft tie, such as pantyhose, around the trunk of the tree in a figure eight pattern.

When using stakes to secure large transplants, short thick stakes are ideal. These are hammered into the ground around the tree as anchorage points for guy ropes. When trees are staked in this way it may be necessary to protect the tree trunk by encasing the guy ropes in hose or by wrapping the trunk with hessian.

The plant tie will need to be able to be adjusted as the plant grows to allow for the increased diameter of the trunk. The area under the tie or between the stake and the trunk should be checked regularly for pests such as scale or mealy bug, and to ensure that there is no damage being caused to the plant by rubbing or friction between the stake and the stem.

While a length of hardwood, bamboo or metal (such as a star picket) is commonly used as a stake, it is also possible to buy ornamental stakes or plant supports. These turn a functional item into a garden decoration. Wooden stakes can also be painted to reduce their impact in the garden. Green or black stakes tend to disappear into the background.

You can also utilise strong straight prunings from established garden plants. Traditional plants that are used in this way include hazel and bamboo but any strong, straight length of stem can be used as a stake.

Checking stakes and ties

Where stakes have been used to secure a plant, it is important to regularly check the stake and its ties. Make sure the stake is firmly fixed in the ground and that ties are secure but not cutting into the plant. If necessary, loosen the tie to avoid damage. Without regular attention, plant ties can damage the plant they are meant to support by cutting into bark or distorting growth.

If a plant has been staked for only temporary support, remove the stakes and ties as soon as possible.

Stakes and plant ties can also provide sheltered spots for pests to hide or

RIGHT Pantyhose, being soft and cheap, works well as a plant tie.

OPPOSITE To avoid root damage, always insert the stake at planting time. Position it close to the main trunk, using a tie with an adjustable strap.

congregate in. Regularly check these areas and remove or treat any pests. Scale, mealy bug and caterpillars can hide on or beneath plant ties or between the plant's trunk and the stake.

Stakes can also be a danger to gardeners. Covering the top of the stake with an upside-down empty pot or tennis ball can prevent eye damage if you are gardening in or around stakes. Always remove broken or damaged stakes as these too can be a hazard that can lead to injury. Old stakes should not be re-used as they may be harbouring pests that could potentially reinfest subsequent crops.

Special needs for transplants

Plants that have been dug up and moved from one area to another need regular attention and care in the days, weeks and months after they've been transplanted. If the weather is particularly hot or dry, provide transplants with additional water and if possible shade to reduce transpiration.

Caring for established plants

In most cases, as plants grow both below and above ground, the intensive care that was required after planting can be gradually reduced. With plants that are growing well and that suit the climate and soil, little care may be needed. For most garden plants, ongoing care usually takes the form of an occasional watering (particularly when conditions are unseasonably dry or extremely hot), the application of fertiliser at the beginning of a plant's growth cycle (normally in spring but occasionally in summer or autumn), topping up of mulches once or twice a year, and the removal of weeds. Plants should also be checked for pests and diseases. As plants grow it may be necessary to prune them to contain their growth, shape them or to encourage flowering or fruiting. Climbing plants may need to be tied on to a trellis or plant support to keep them in check.

Where plants have been placed too closely together it may be necessary to remove some plants to provide better growing conditions for neighbouring plants. Hedge plants that have been planted too closely together may need to be pruned or it may be necessary to remove every second plant in a row. Also check plants that are growing beside walls or built structures, as pests may congregate on the protected side of the plant where they may breed undetected.

FAR LEFT Remove nursery stakes, ties and plant labels at the time of planting.
LEFT A cut-down tennis ball slipped over the top of a garden stake will protect you and others.
OPPOSITE Train climbing plants onto and up a trellis by regularly tying new stems.

CHAPTER 10

Tools of the trade

Why do I need to read this chapter?

- To discover what tools are needed for which task in your garden.

- For a basic tool list to get you started in your garden.

- To learn how to care for and store tools.

Getting started in the garden

Tools make gardening tasks easier and more efficient. There's a limit to what you can achieve in a garden simply using your bare hands! However, a new gardener needs only a few basic tools to get started.

Garden tools can be divided broadly into hand tools and power tools. Hand tools require physical energy and are used for most basic garden tasks such as digging, raking, hoeing and pruning. Power tools, usually powered by petrol, battery or electrical current, are used for repetitive tasks such a mowing, hedging or cutting timber, or for heavy or complex tasks.

Buying hand tools

It is easy to be overwhelmed by the sheer number and variety of tools on offer. There is also a huge price variation, reflecting the quality, materials and place of manufacture.

Most hand tools are made from anodised or powder-coated steel, with a polycarbonate or fibreglass handle. Some are brightly coloured, making them more visible in the garden so they won't be lost or accidentally tripped over. Many are also light and easy to use. Be careful when buying some cheaper tools. Many are not made to last and cannot be repaired.

Recycled options

If you are on a tight budget but want to own good quality garden tools, consider buying those that are second-hand and in fair condition. For those concerned about the hidden environmental costs of manufactured goods, second-hand tools also tick the eco-friendly box.

Ask older friends and relations who may have assembled a collection of garden tools if they have any they would like to pass on. You may find unused tools that can be repaired or they may agree to swap their older tools for lightweight modern ones that are more suited to their current garden needs.

Old garden tools (and expensive modern tools) are manufactured from forged steel and hardwood. Handles are made from ash, cherry, elm, yew and other hardwoods, or from metal. Many of the tools from yesteryear were hand forged by blacksmiths.

When buying second-hand tools, check for strength and test the tools in exactly the same way that you would if you were buying a new tool. A tool shouldn't be too heavy for you to use and it should be of a suitable length for you to work with comfortably.

ABOVE A hand trowel is useful for digging up small weeds and grass runners.

Tools for tools

As well as garden tools, gardeners need a range of associated tools to help care for and maintain their implements. Maintenance may include sharpening of blades, replacing springs or repairs to handles or attachments. Equipment that may be needed for tool maintenance includes a workbench, vice, chisels, saw, angle grinder and whetstones (for sharpening secateurs and other cutting blades). If you don't have this equipment (or don't have space to house it) you can get tools sharpened and repaired at some hardware stores and specialist lawn mower centres.

Just because a tool is old and cheap, it doesn't necessarily follow that it is a good buy. Before you buy an old tool or spend money restoring it, make sure you check it thoroughly for rust, dents and damage to the edge of blades, and any other signs of damage. For gardeners who like old-style tools, there are specialist manufacturers who are making reproductions of some of these. They are available from specialist garden shops and by mail order.

Tip Many handles are broken when tools are misused. Don't use a spade as a prising or leveraging tool as it is likely the handle will snap. If you are trying to prise rocks from your garden or remove long-rooted weeds, use a crowbar, a mattock or a pick, not a spade.

Replacing tool handles

You may look at a handle and think it is damaged beyond repair and impossible to replace, but most older style tools can be repaired. If you have a modern tool, contact the manufacturer to discover whether there are replacement parts available.

The job of replacing a tool handle or head can be fiddly and requires specialist tools. For example, if the handle is riveted on to the metal head, an angle grinder is needed to remove the rivets.

The task may involve work and specialist tools, but it is well worth replacing damaged tool handles if the business end is still serviceable. For a little work you can save 60–80 per cent of the cost of buying the tool new. Replacement wooden handles for various tools generally cost $10–$20. Look for good quality replacement wooden handles.

To remove the old handle, use a hacksaw or grinder to shear off the head of the nail holding it in place. Using a punch, hammer the body of the nail further into the handle and

Tip If the handle is broken and tricky to remove, use heat as a last resort. Warm the spade head up in an oven to loosen. When it cools enough to be comfortably handled, remove it with a chisel.

then slide off the tool head. With a chisel or plane, and sandpaper, adjust the end of the new handle until it fits into the tool head. Slide it into the tool head and twist to tighten. Fasten the handle to the tool head by hammering in a flat head nail.

Removing a riveted wooden tool handle

Here are some tips on how to remove a wooden handle that has been attached by rivets. You'll need an angle grinder, punch and hammer, pliers, vice, drill and drill bits.

Firstly, using an angle grinder, remove the head of the rivets. Use a punch to remove the remains of the rivets and pull them out with a pair of pliers.

If the remains of the wooden handle are still resistant and not coming out easily, put the tool head so it is held securely (for example in a vice) and drill into the wood to remove it.

To secure the replacement handle in the tool head, drill the holes a little deeper and use a screw or flat head nail instead of rivets.

Spade or a shovel?

You've probably heard the old saying about a straight talking person—they call a spade a spade. In most cases the tool that gardeners call a spade is actually a shovel. They differ in both their shape and purpose.

A spade is a digging tool. It has a straight or curved sharp edge that should be kept sharpened. A spade usually has a straight handle. It is used to dig soil, make a planting hole and drainage holes or to incorporate organic matter into soil. Spades may have a D-shaped handle or a bar handle (also known as a T-handle). The choice really is a matter of individual preference. Try both options and select the one you feel is easiest to use.

A shovel, by contrast, is a tool that shifts and lifts. Shovels are particularly useful for moving soil, mulch or other material. They have a broad flat edge to allow you to scoop or lift material. Don't use a shovel to dig holes—they'll make it hard work! Shovels also have different options for the shape of the handle with either a D-shaped handle or T-handle. Try out the feel of the shovel before you buy.

Both are useful tools to have in your collection, but if you can only have one to start off your collection, it is best to choose a good spade.

RIGHT This spade is being used correctly as a digging tool.

Dirty dozen

These are the essential tools to get you started digging, planting, watering and maintaining your garden efficiently.

Spade	Loppers
Fork	Saw
Rake	Hose and fittings
Trowel	Bucket
Hoe	Watering can
Secateurs	Lawn mower

Making it easy

There are ergonomic tools available, designed with function and ease of use in mind. There are also many tools that have been designed for people who have disabilities, or who are smaller or not as strong as most. There are also tools designed specifically for children. Some ergonomic tools are available from hardware stores but others have to be sourced from specialist suppliers such as horticultural therapists.

Tools are also available with handles that can be easily adjusted to suit the height of the user. Also look for mechanisms such as ratchets that need less energy to operate. Pruners and loppers in particular are easier to use with ratchet handles.

LEFT Shovels have a broad, flat edge that makes them useful for lifting and shifting material such as compost and mulch.

Spade Used to dig holes, turn soil. Select the length and shape of handle that suits your height, hand size and ability. If two people of different heights are using the same spade, look for one with an adjustable handle that can be made longer or shorter.

Fork Used to lift and toss materials and break up clods. It is also handy for separating plants during propagation and for aerating soil.

Rake A metal-tined rake is used to rake gravel, level soil and remove stones from soil prior to planting. A plastic long-tined rake is better for raking leaves, but you should use a metal long-tined rake for removing thatch from lawns.

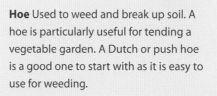

Trowel Used for digging, planting and transplanting small plants and removing weeds. Trowels can be made of polymer, metal or wood.

Hoe Used to weed and break up soil. A hoe is particularly useful for tending a vegetable garden. A Dutch or push hoe is a good one to start with as it is easy to use for weeding.

Secateurs Used to cut and prune plants with branch diameter up to 20–25 mm. They are also used to take cuttings for propagation.

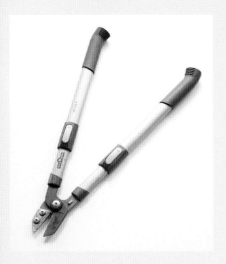

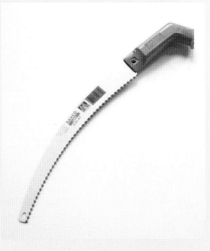

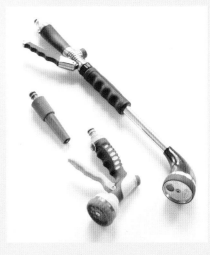

Loppers Used to cut or prune hard and to lop thick material that the secateurs can't manage (up to 40 mm thick). For added value, look for loppers with a ratchet mechanism. This provides even more leverage and makes cutting through thick stems easy work.

Saw Used to cut branches and prune thick material. Choose a pruning saw if you have roses or fruit trees that need regular pruning, but if you are clearing a lot of overgrown plants you may need a bow saw or even a small chainsaw as well.

Hose with fittings Used to water the garden, and the attachments allow you to add a sprinkler. A hose is also useful for laying out guidelines when designing a garden bed.

Watering can Used to carry water, water potted plants, apply fertilisers and chemicals. Plastic watering cans are lighter and easier to manage but not as durable as metal cans.

Lawn mower The most commonly used push lawn mowers are rotary mowers. They include hand-powered and petrol-powered models. Petrol mowers have either a two-stroke or four-stroke motor.

Bucket Used to carry water, soil, compost or other materials. Buckets are also useful for dunking small pot plants prior to planting or for collecting produce.

Adding to your tool collection

In addition to the 12 basic garden tools outlined on the preceding pages, gardeners need to acquire tools depending on the nature of their garden. For example, if you are starting a garden from scratch, or have stones to move, you may need a crowbar and pick. However, you may not need these tools in a well-established garden.

If you have vast areas of lawns, you'll need to invest in tools such as an edger, weeder and perhaps a line trimmer (best known as a whipper snipper or Strimmer) to help maintain the lawn and keep it neat and tidy.

It's also good idea to have basic spare parts, such as plugs and blades for the mower (for more on lawn mower maintenance see page 164) and line for the line trimmer, close to hand. New parts can take some time to acquire, and you don't want to be held up in the middle of your job waiting for parts to arrive.

If you have extensive hedges, you'll need a petrol-powered or electric hedge trimmer. To undertake fine pruning invest in good hedge shears with a wavy blade. To prune hard-to-reach branches without needing to climb a ladder include a pole pruner in your tool collection.

RIGHT A wheelbarrow is perfect for transporting compost and soil.

Tip Some pruning tools have interchangeable heads, such as shears and saw attachments. These make tools much more versatile and also save space as they are easier to store.

To make your own compost or mulch add a compost bin, along with a shredder or mulcher, to your tool purchases. If you need to transport loads, you will need to add a wheelbarrow and a shovel to your list, so you can easily move materials such as mulch or soil. And, if your garden is small with narrow paths, you may need to select a smaller wheelbarrow rather than a larger one. In short, every individual gardener and garden will have their own unique requirements for their tools and equipment.

Specialist garden tools
Specialist garden tools have evolved with gardening. The following tools are useful additions to your shed.
A: Cloche A clear cover placed over small plants to protect them from adverse conditions, such as cold or frost.
B: Dibbler Used to make small holes in soil or potting mix for planting seeds or seedlings.
C: Whetstone A stone used to sharpen small blades.
D: Budding knife Used in plant propagation techniques such as grafting and budding.

Step-by-Step

HOW TO SHARPEN SECATEURS

1   Loosen the bolt with a spanner.

2   Completely take apart the secateurs.

3   Sharpen the blade with a whetstone or steel. Hold it at the same angle as the bevelled edge and draw it along the edge, sharpening away from your body. Remove any built-up resin with a wire brush, steel wool or fine sandpaper.

4   Oil the blades, spring and nut and bolt. Reassemble the secateurs.

Tip Looking like an oversized corkscrew, the 'compost worm' tool is handy to have to help aerate the compost inside a compost bin.

RIGHT To maintain a wooden handle, rub it down with steel wool or sandpaper, then condition with linseed oil.
OPPOSITE A flexible plastic bucket or trug is a handy way to carry tools needed for a day's activity in the garden.

Caring for tools

Tools work better and last longer when they are well cared for. It's best to store tools in a shed, where they are protected from the elements.

Sometimes tools are left outside inadvertently as they are hard to see among garden plants, soils and mulches. It's a good idea to mark their handles with reflective tape or bright paint that is easy to spot against the greenery. This also prevents tools being accidentally tossed into the compost bin or the rubbish when you are cleaning up.

It is easier to gather tools up after you've finished gardening if you have them in a container such a wheelbarrow (especially good to cart large tools) or a bucket (for small tools). Alternatively, invest in a garden caddy or tool belt to hold and transport tools that are needed for specific gardening jobs so you have them on hand as required.

After use, tools should be cleaned and put away. Cleaning only takes a

ABOVE Sinking metal blades into a mix of sand and oil helps to prevent them rusting.

few moments and usually involves removing dirt or plant sap from the cutting edges of spades, lawn mower blades or secateurs. Large tools can be washed down under a tap or with a hose and then thoroughly dried. Stubborn dirt can be removed with a wire brush. The blades of smaller tools such as secateurs should be wiped clean with a cloth and then oiled.

Blades and handles

If you have used tools to remove or prune diseased plants, sterilise the blades by wiping them over with disinfectant or diluted bleach. Blades can also be rubbed with oil such as machinery oil to stop them rusting. If there is dry resin or sap on any blade, remove it with fine sandpaper, steel wool or a wire brush. A wire brush will remove rust on carbon steel blades such as spades or hoes.

Keeping your blades sharp will maintain their effectiveness. If the blade of your spade or hoe becomes blunt, use a grinder or a file to sharpen the cutting edge. Wear safety glasses or a safety mask to protect you from injury that may be caused by flying particles when using a grinder.

Blunt blades, particularly on secateurs, can damage plants and may make them more vulnerable to fungal or bacterial infection. These blades can be sharpened on a whetstone or with a sharpening stone or special sharpening tool for that brand. Some models can be taken apart so blades can be replaced (see 'How to sharpen secateurs', page 161). The cutting edge of a spade can be sharpened with a grinder.

Keep wooden handles of spades, forks and rakes in good condition by regularly rubbing them with oil. A mix made of equal parts of linseed oil and mineral turpentine is easy to prepare at home and to apply to the handle with an old cloth.

Step-by-Step

RESTORING HANDLES

1 Clean off any soil from the handle, then sand away any roughness using medium grade sandpaper.

2 To nourish and preserve the wood, wipe the handle with a mix of linseed oil and turpentine. Rub it in with a cloth. Leave to dry.

3 If the handle is still rough, smooth it over with fine grade sandpaper and reapply the linseed oil and turpentine mix.

4 Finish by polishing the handle with steel wool.

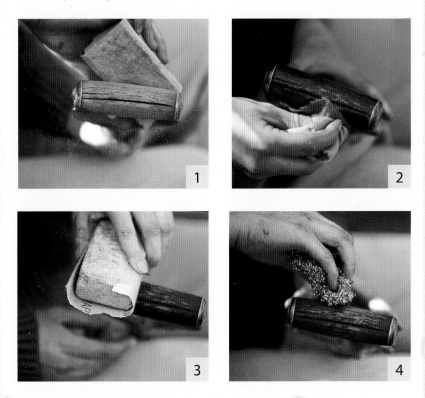

Tip A mixture of linseed oil and turpentine will help to preserve wooden handles and shafts of tools.

Mower maintenance

- In a four-stroke lawn mower, check oil level and oil colour. This task is often neglected by gardeners. Top up the oil if necessary and change it when it is dirty (black). As oil quickly becomes dirty with regular use of the mower, change the oil around every six months.
- Check spark plugs (right). Dirty spark plugs are the main reason a mower doesn't start first go, so regularly check the spark plug in your mower, examining for carbon build-up. This can be cleaned with a wire brush or replaced if necessary.

- Check blades. Blades become worn and nicked with use. Regularly replace blades so the mower cuts rather than rips the grass. Before working on the mower remove the spark plug to disable the blades. Replace the bolts at the same time as you replace the blades. When checking or replacing blades on a four-stroke mower, don't upend it. Instead, tilt it on its side, with the carburettor on the higher side, so oil doesn't run into the carburettor. After use, remove any build-up of lawn clippings or dirt from the blades by giving it a quick hose or brushing down.
- Fuel levels. Don't put the lawn mower away for a long period of time with fuel left in the tank. Keep the mower running until all the fuel is used. Old fuel in the tank can make a lawn mower hard to restart.

Caring for tools with moving parts

The moving parts on hand tools such as secateurs, loppers, shears and sprayers should be given a squirt of oil at least once a year or after heavy use.

The teeth on the chains on chainsaws should be sharpened after heavy use with an electric chain-sharpening tool (available at hardware stores or done by your chainsaw specialist). The chain will wear away over time and will need replacing when it becomes too worn to be sharpened. This task is best done at a repair centre.

Lawn mowers

Lawn mowers that get regular maintenance last longer and always start first go. As lawn mowers are used throughout most of the year but more often in summer when grass is growing vigorously, it is best to service your lawn mower at the beginning of the cutting season (in spring) and then again during summer.

You can take your lawn mower to a specialist who can undertake maintenance, but mower care is straightforward if you have the correct resources. Keep a spare air filter element, spark plugs and blades in the tool shed so you can service your mower easily and efficiently at home. To undertake your own maintenance follow the tips in 'Mower maintenance', left. Select a clean, well-lit spot in which to work.

Storing tools

Store your garden tools in a dry and secure place to keep them in good condition and safe from being lost or stolen. Tools that are exposed to water or even damp may rust, rot or become brittle. Plastic tools, in particular, become brittle if exposed to ultra-violet light so store these out of the sunlight. It pays to clean and oil tools before storing them for any length of time. This is easily done; mix some vegetable oil into a small bucket of washed sand and then dip the tool into the bucket a few times. Any soil or grime will be cleaned off and the surface coated with oil to prevent rust.

Hanging tools up on a wall in your shed, garage or laundry is a good storage option. Not only are they secure, but they will also be easy to find when needed. You can make your own supports to store tools safely by hammering nails into a wall, setting up a pegboard or by buying and installing a tool storage system from a storage specialist or hardware store.

Using tools safely

When you are using tools keep safety in mind—for yourself and those around you. Have appropriate safety gear handy and wear it.

When you are mowing or digging in the garden, wear solid shoes, preferably boots. Gaiters that slip over the top of work boots help keep grass and debris from falling into your boots.

If you are using a tool that is likely to throw up small fragments or stones, wear eye protection and keep others (including pets) away as you work. Lawn mowers, line trimmers and grinders can all send small pieces flying, and that can be dangerous. Avoid potential problems by walking over an area to be mowed removing fallen sticks, children's toys, wire, rope, the garden hose, stones and other hard objects.

Also be aware of sparks from tools, especially in times of high fire danger as a single spark can start a fire that could get out of control.

Electrical cords are another hazard outdoors. If you are using a tool with an electrical cord make sure you know where the cord is and keep it away from blades. Avoid using extension cords wherever possible but if it is unavoidable, ensure that you use one that is rated for outdoor use. Don't use electrical tools or extension cords in the rain or near water. To avoid any chance of electrocution make sure a surge arrestor is installed for your

power supply to instantly cut off power if there is an accident. While these safety devices are mandatory in new homes they may need to be installed in older dwellings. so check your power box.

One of the most dangerous of all garden tools, however, has no moving parts, sparks or electrical power. Falls from ladders are the most common garden accident and can be fatal. Don't climb a ladder if you don't need to. If

ABOVE A ladder is one of the most dangerous tools in the garden. Always ensure it is secure.

you have to use a ladder, make sure it is securely positioned so it can't slip or wobble and don't climb above the top step. Have someone with you for extra safety. Don't lean out. If you cannot reach without leaning, get down and move the ladder.

Glossary

There are many specialist terms you are likely to encounter when you garden and grow plants. Here's a list of some of the words or terms you'll find in this book and in other garden-related media along with a basic explanation of what each word means in the world of gardening and plants.

Note Words within the definition in **bold** are also included in the glossary.

Annual Plants, usually seed grown, which complete their life cycle in one growing season.

Anti-transpirant A chemical applied to foliage to reduce moisture loss by **transpiration** and often applied to protect transplants. Can also protect plants from frost damage.

Bacillus thuringiensis A naturally occurring bacteria used to kill caterpillars that turn into moths or butterflies. Referred to as Bt.

Bare rooted Plants with an exposed root system and not presented for sale grown in a pot. Usually applied to plants such as roses, fruit trees and vines sold during their dormant period when they can be transplanted. Roots are usually protected from desiccation by being wrapped in sphagnum or coir peat and contained in a plastic, paper or hessian sleeve or wrap.

Beer trap A trap baited with beer to attract snails and slugs. Usually a tin, jar or saucer set into the ground so snails and slugs fall in and can't crawl out.

Biennial Plants that take two growing seasons to complete their life cycle (that is growing, flowering, seeding). Some edible plants that are biennial are grown as annuals as they can be harvested before they flower. Examples of commonly grown biennials include aquilegia, foxglove and parsley.

Bolting Going to seed prematurely, usually applied to herbs or vegetables. Bolting can be caused by water or heat stress. When edible plants shift from vegetative growth to flowering and seeding their leaves often become bitter and inedible.

Broadcast Scattering seeds or fertiliser over the ground.

Bulb A fleshy storage organ, technically a swollen root; also used to describe a plant that's grown from bulb or **corm**.

Carbon sink Term used to describe elements of the environment such as plants and soil that store carbon.

Check When growth suddenly slows. Usually due to cold or heat but also caused by lack of water or nourishment.

Cloche A plant cover (traditionally a bell-shaped glass) used as temporary protection against frost and cold. Plastic containers such as milk or juice bottles with their bases removed can be used instead of traditional glass cloches.

Clump Describes the way a plant grows to form a mass of leaves and roots. Grasses, lilies and plants with rhizomes often form a clump as they grow. These clumps can be split up by **dividing**.

Cold frame Low structure with solid walls and a glass or plastic removable lid or cover used to protect plants over winter or during propagation.

Compaction Firming of soil, soils that lack porosity (air). Compacted soils are often detrimental for plant growth.

Companion planting Growing compatible plants together for pollination, pest control or shelter.

Compost Decomposed organic matter or the act of creating decomposed organic matter in a compost heap or bin. In the UK the term compost also refers to **potting mix**.

LEFT A compost bin neatly contains decomposing organic matter as it forms compost.

Cover crop Grown to protect fallow or uncultivated soil during winter. See also **Green manure**.

Crop rotation The planned switching of crops from the same plant family to different growing areas to avoid soil-borne pests and diseases and the depletion of soil nutrients.

Cross-pollination The transference of pollen from one plant to another, usually from one variety to another. Some plants cannot be fertilised with their own pollen or with that of the same variety so, for fruit formation, a compatible pollen source is required. It is important for fruit production.

Crown The growth point of herbaceous plants from which new shoots appear. On a tree, the crown is the leafy part at the top of the trunk.

Cutting A piece of a plant used for propagation. Also called a slip.

Compost tea A form of liquid fertiliser made by steeping compost in water, straining and applying to plants to provide nutrients.

Contact insecticide A chemical used to kill insects when it comes into contact with them.

Coppice Hard pruning to ground level to encourage trees or shrubs to reshoot from roots or lignotubers. Often done to manage woodland areas, keep trees compact or to encourage immature foliage.

Corm A swollen underground stem.

Damping off A disease that can kill young seedlings at or prior to germination. Fungal pathogens that leading to damping off include botrytis, rhizoctonia and pythium. It can be prevented through planting in a sterile, dryer environment.

ABOVE An espaliered plum tree.
OPPOSITE A deciduous Japanese maple.

Deadheading Removing spent flowers. This is done to tidy a plant, to stop it seeding, to encourage more buds to form, or to remove a source of disease or pests.

Deciduous A type of plant that discards all its leaves. This usually occurs in autumn and winter with regrowth of new leaves during spring. Some plants are dry season deciduous, which means they lose their leaves during the dry season and re-leaf as the wet season approaches.

Deficiency The lack of an essential nutrients required for growth.

Dibble To make a hole for planting using a dibbler or dibber, a solid, often wooden, tool. Also called dibbing.

Divide/division Terms used to describe plant propagation done by splitting a large **clump** to form several sections, each of which can become a new plant.

Dormant Not actively growing. In cold climates many plants become dormant during winter but plants may also be dormant at other times of the year.

Drench To thoroughly wet soil or **potting mix**. A **pesticide, fungicide** or **herbicide** applied to wet a plant and/or the soil.

Espalier The art of training a plant so its branches grow flat against a support, such as a wall. This is achieved by the removal of outward growing branches and the training of horizontal branches, by being tied to horizontal supports such as wires or a lattice. Espaliers can form shapes such as fans. While espaliers are ornamental, espalier work also allows a plant to be grown in a narrow space and in a microclimate that may be warmer than the surrounding area.

RIGHT Legumes form nodules on their roots.
OPPOSITE Mulch conserves soil moisture.

Evergreen A plant that retains its leaves year round.

Fertiliser Any substance that contains plant nutrients such as nitrogen, phosphorus and potassium. Fertilisers come in many different forms.

Foliar fertiliser A liquid fertiliser that's applied to the leaves of a plant so it is absorbed via the leaf tissue rather than the roots. Foliar fertilisers are useful when plants are drought or cold stressed, or have a nutrient **deficiency** as they can readily absorb nutrients.

Friable A term used to describe soil which is easy to dig, well drained and without clods. Friable soil can be created by digging soil thoroughly and incorporating organic matter.

Fungicide A garden chemical used to treat fungal disease. Often based on copper or sulfur.

Garden centre A retail **nursery**. Usually a business that resells plants and other garden-related items but doesn't grow its own plants.

Germination When a seed shoots and begins to grow. The new plant is called a **seedling**.

Glut A surfeit of one type of crop that occurs when fruit or vegetables all ripen at the same time. See also **Staggered planting**.

Glyphosate A broad spectrum herbicide used to control weeds.

Graft The point at which one plant (a **scion**) is joined to another (**understock**). Also called graft union.

Green manure A **cover crop** that is grown to flowering then dug back into the soil to add nutrients. Leguminous crops such as peas and vetch in particular are grown to add nitrogen to soils. See also **Legume.**

Gypsum A soft mineral (calcium sulfate dihydrate) applied to hard-to-cultivate clay soils to improve water penetration.

Hardening-off Acclimatising a plant to new usually harsher growing conditions such as occurs when a newly propagated plant is moved from a sheltered growing area to the garden or when an indoor plant is moved into more light outdoors.

Hardy A plant that's able to cope with adverse conditions such as cold, heat or drought. In cold climates, hardy plants are generally those that are cold or frost tolerant. In warm climates hardy plants are considered tolerant of drought.

nurseries often specialise in rare or unusual plants. Stock is usually delivered by post or courier directly to the gardener and often is only available seasonally—for example when the plant is **dormant**.

Micro-irrigation Small sprays attached to a fixed irrigation or watering system.

Mulch A loose organic or inorganic material spread over the ground around plants to suppress weed growth, reduce moisture loss and protect the soil from heat. Organic mulches decompose to add nutrients to soil.

Mushroom compost The organic material available after a crop of commercially grown mushrooms has been harvested. It can be added to soil as a **soil conditioner** or used as **mulch**. Mushroom compost can be highly alkaline. It is available direct from mushroom growers or from landscape suppliers or in bags from **nurseries**.

Node The growth point on a stem.

Nursery A business that grows or sells plants. A nursery that grows plants and sells them on to a **garden centre** is referred to as a wholesale nursery. Whatever businesses may not sell directly to wholesale businesses.

Heavy soils Clay-based soils that are poorly drained and difficult to dig.

Herbaceous perennial A plant that dies down each year and has a period of **dormancy**, usually over winter but sometimes over summer, and re-grows as the weather warms in spring, or rain falls in autumn. See also **Perennial**.

Herbicide A chemical that kills plants and particularly used to kill weeds. See also **Glyphosate**.

Knocking out Taking a plant out of its pot. Plants can usually be removed more easily if the side of the pot is tapped or knocked to separate the root ball from the side and bottom of the container.

Larva The juvenile form of an insect such as a butterfly, moth or fly before pupation. Plural larvae.

Legume Any plant that forms nodules on its roots that allow atmospheric nitrogen to be incorporated into soils. Peas and beans are legumes.

Liquid feed A water-soluble fertiliser; the application of a liquid fertiliser.

Mail-order nursery A business that sells plants through advertisements, mailing lists or websites. Mail-order

Nymph An immature life stage of an insect such as a bug or beetle.

Organic gardening Gardening without applying dangerous chemicals and with an overwhelming concern for the environment.

Oversow, oversowing Scattering seed over an area already planted, such as a lawn or garden bed. Lawns are often oversown with grass seed to cover gaps or provide growth when the main lawn grass variety is dormant.

Parterre A garden bed planted to form a pattern using low-growing or clipped plants.

Perennial A plant that grows year after year. Usually used to describe smaller, clump-forming plants with soft growth. The perennial category is further divided into herbaceous **(herbaceous perennial)**, which refers to plants that die down each year and reshoot, usually in spring, and evergreen, which refers to clump-forming plants that stay leafy all year round.

Perlite A lightweight aggregate made from rock and often added to potting or propagating mixes.

Pesticide A chemical product used to kill insect pests. Pesticides may be formulated as **systemic** or **contac**t.

They are sold as concentrates, which must be mixed with water before use or as ready-to-use products. Each pesticide container carries a label, which includes vital information about the use of the product including the active ingredient, application rates and safety measures.

Pheromone A chemical scent produced by insects and animals to attract others particularly for mating. Pheromones are used to trap insects by acting as a lure.

Pinching Removing soft shoots or buds using fingers rather than secateurs. Also called pinching out.

pH A measure of hydrogen ions in soil or water. A scale from 0–14 is used to indicate the degree of acidity or alkalinity where 7 is neutral. pH can be measured using a test kit, probe or meter available from nurseries, hardware stores or specialist instrument suppliers.

Pollination Transfer of pollen (the male part of the flower) to form fruit. See also **Cross-pollination.**

Porosity Generally referring to the ability of soil to hold air and water.

Potager A vegetable or herb garden laid out in an ornamental fashion.

Potting mix A growing medium usually based on composted bark and formulated for use in containers. Potting mixes usually contain no soil. Also called a soilless mix.

Potting on Transferring a plant from one pot to another, larger pot.

Propagate/propagation To grow a new plant from another by seed or by cloning methods (also called asexual propagation) such as by **cutting**, **division**, **grafting** or budding or from tissue culture.

Prune To cut back a plant to create a more desirable shape, encourage new growth, particularly to promote flowering, or remove dead or diseased plant material.

Punnet A small container usually around 15 cm long and 10 cm wide that may be divided into cells. Used to grow seedlings. Seedlings are sold by the punnet by nurseries.

Raised bed A garden bed made higher than the surrounding soil level. It may be created by edging or enclosing all sides to hold extra soil. Raised beds are recommended for planting to avoid drainage problems in heavy or poorly drained soils, where the soil lacks depth or where digging is too difficult to undertake.

ABOVE A potager.

Revert A plant that has exhibited a fancy growth form returns to a plainer form—often that of its parent.

Rhizome Swollen underground stem that gives rise to roots and shoots. Often found in perennial plants.

Root-bound A root system that is congested within a pot. Also known as pot bound. Root pruning may repair the damage but root-bound plants often fail to thrive unless transplanted.

Root control bag A textile bag used to contain a root system in the ground where plants are to be transplanted.

Rooting hormone Substances known as auxins that encourage plants to form root growth instead of shoot growth. Used to stimulate **cuttings** to form roots. They are available as powders or gels and sold at most nurseries and hardware stores.

Secateurs Hand tool with cutting blades, used in the garden to cut or prune. Blades may be bypass (cutting like scissors) or anvil (one sharp blade cutting against a blunt edge).

Seed A plant embryo, often encased in a pod or fruit.

Seed potato A tuber from which new potatoes are grown.

Seed saving Collecting and storing seed for replanting.

LEFT Succulents are often drought-hardy.

Seedling A small, immature plant grown from seed.

Setting The formation of **seed** (or fruit) after flowering when pollination has occurred.

Side dressing Applications of fertiliser beside existing plants. Side dressing is often applied to rows of vegetables during their growing period.

Slips Cuttings.

Soaker hose A hose with holes at intervals that slowly emit water. Also known as a weep hose.

Soil conditioner Any organic material added to soil to improve its nutrient content and ability to hold water.

Soil-wetting agent A substance closely allied to detergent that alters the nature of the surface of soil to allow water to penetrate. See also **Wetting agents**.

Sport A spontaneous growth that is different from other parts of a plant. Has the potential to give rise to a new variety. For example it may have variegated leaves or differently coloured blooms.

Staggered planting The sowing of **seed** or **seedlings** over a period of weeks so crops mature at different times. Usually done in vegetable planting to avoid a **glut**.

Standard A plant trained or grafted so that it has a long, straight stem topped with a ball of growth.

Standard potting mix A **potting mix** that meets the Australian Standard.

Stopping Pruning off the growing tip—often by **pinching** or **tip pruning**—to encourage side branches.

Succulent A fleshy plant, often drought-hardy.

Suckers Shoots that arise from a root or system. See also **Understock**.

Systemic A pesticide taken into the plant's sap. When insects feed on stems, flowers or foliage or sap they are killed. Some **fungicides** may also be systemic and so deter fungal growth.

Terrarium A clear container (usually glass or plastic) that can be sealed or open to provide a humid growing space for plants.

Thinning out Removing excess seedlings in a row to allow those remaining adequate growing space.

The term may also be used to refer to pruning to reduce the canopy of a tree or shrub or the removal of buds or small fruit within a cluster.

Top dressing Applying a thin layer of organic matter or fertiliser to soil beside or in the case of lawns over existing plants.

Topiary The art of clipping plants into shapes or the shaped plant itself.

Top soil The top layer of soil which is usually rich in organic matter and nutrients.

Training The use of pruning and the tying of plants to supports such as stakes or trellises to control their shape, size and form.

Transplant A plant that is moved from one location to another by being dug up or the act of digging up and replanting.

Variegated/variegation A leaf or petal that shows one or more colours often in attractive patterns. Plants with variegated leaves or flowers are often highly desirable. The variegated patterns may be naturally occurring or be induced by virus infection or exposure to chemicals. Plants that are variegated may **revert** to plain growth.

Vermiculite Expanded mica, commonly used in pots or for **propagation**, due to its light weight and inert properties.

Water crystals A polymer-based commercial product that holds water. They are often added to commercial **potting mixes** and can be added to soils and potting mixes to reduce moisture stress in plants. See also **Soil-wetting agent**.

Water-repellent soils Soils or **potting mixes** that fail to absorb moisture as applied moisture runs off rather than soaking in. Such soils are often very sandy or lacking in organic matter. **Potting mixes** that dry out completely may be hard to re-wet. See also **Soil-wetting agent, Water crystals**.

Wetting agents Substances related to detergents that are added to chemicals such as **pesticides, fungicides** or **herbicides** to assist their penetration of the leaf surface. See also **Soil-wetting agent**.

Wind rock Damage caused to plants, particularly trees and **transplants**, when buffeted by wind causing their roots to become loose in the soil. Wind rock can kill or seriously impede plant growth. Staking and pruning are techniques used to reduce wind rock.

Index

Acknowledgements

A book like this takes lots of time to create and impinges on day to day life and particularly family time so we want to say thanks to our families for their help, support and advice while we were both hard at work on this book. So thank you to: Kiera Beauman, Margery and John Postlethwaite, Greg Prentice, Helen Stackhouse, Shirley and John Stackhouse, and Jim, Rowan and Eleanor Taylor. Where would we be with out you!

Also a 'Thanks guys!' to our colleagues on ABC *Gardening Australia* magazine: Anna, Frank, Gina, Jenny, Justin, Kate, Lili, Susan and Susan.

Jennifer and Debbie

Picture credits

All photographs by Ian Hoffstetter, except for the following:

123RF.com: page 75

Brett Stevens: page 66

Garden World Images: page 88E

iStockphoto: Front cover: Lydia Goolia; Back cover: Lehner (left), Kkgas (right); pages 38, 56, 82D, 116, 136, 138, 176

Living Holmes Design: page 127

Murdoch Books Photo Library / Joe Filshie: pages 8, 76, 101, 109, 110

Murdoch Books Photo Library / Lorna Rose: pages 25, 30, 32, 35, 39, 40, 81, 83A, 88A, 88C, 88D, 89, 91, 93, 94, 96, 106, 108, 111, 170-172, 423

Murdoch Books Photo Library / Sue Stubbs: pages 12, 14, 34, 51, 59, 65, 68, 78-80, 82A-C, 82E, 83B-D, 88B, 122, 124, 129-135, 150-163

Newslife Media: page 6

Shutterstock: Back cover (middle) Elena Moiseeva; pages 85E, 128

Thinkstock: page 45

About the authors

Jennifer Stackhouse's interest in horticulture and writing was inspired by her family background. After leaving university she began curatorial work at Sydney's Elizabeth Bay House museum, researching the extensive garden that once surrounded the house, and arranging exhibitions of historic plants and heritage roses; it was here that she decided to learn more about plants and gardening. After completing an Associate Diploma in Horticulture, Jennifer joined the staff of the Royal Botanic Gardens, Sydney. She began her career in horticultural media soon afterwards; she currently writes regularly for *Sunday Herald Sun*, *Daily Telegraph* and *Mercury* and other newspapers around Australia and is editor of the well-respected ABC *Gardening Australia* magazine.

Jennifer has a large garden on the outskirts of Sydney, two children, numerous cats, dogs and chooks, and works as an editor, journalist and horticultural consultant.

Debbie McDonald discovered a passion for gardening and sharing the joy of gardens through writing after a short career in the fashion and textile industry. She has been horticultural editor at ABC *Gardening Australia* magazine since 2003, after working for several years as a gardener, garden designer and horticultural consultant. She also edits the magazine of the *Friends of the Botanic Gardens*, Sydney, writes a weekly gardening column in *The Manly Daily*, and loves nothing better than to garden with her young daughter.

Notes

Notes

Notes

Published in 2012 by Murdoch Books Pty Limited

Murdoch Books Australia
Pier 8/9
23 Hickson Road
Millers Point NSW 2000
Phone: +61 (0) 2 8220 2000
Fax: +61 (0) 2 8220 2558
www.murdochbooks.com.au
info@murdochbooks.com.au

Murdoch Books UK Limited
Erico House, 6th Floor
93–99 Upper Richmond Road
Putney, London SW15 2TG
Phone: +44 (0) 20 8785 5995
Fax: +44 (0) 20 8785 5985
www.murdochbooks.co.uk
info@murdochbooks.co.uk

For Corporate Orders & Custom Publishing contact Noel Hammond,
National Business Development Manager Murdoch Books Australia

Chief Executive: Matt Handbury
Publishing Director: Chris Rennie
Publisher: Tracy Lines
Concept Designer: Jacqueline Richards
Layout Designer: Warren Penney
Production: Joan Beal

Text and Design © Murdoch Books Pty Limited 2012
Photography © Murdoch Books Pty Limited 2012

NATIONAL LIBRARY OF AUSTRALIA CIP DATA
Author: Stackhouse, Jennifer
Title: Planting techniques / Jennifer Stackhouse.
ISBN: 9781741967524 (pbk.)
Notes: Includes index.
Subjects: Planting (Plant culture).
Gardening.
Dewey Number: 635

A catalogue record for this book is available from the British Library.

Printed by 1010 Printing International Limited, China

Readers of this book must ensure that any work or project undertaken complies with local
legislative and approval requirements relevant to their particular circumstances. Furthermore,
this work is necessarily of a general nature and cannot be a substitute for appropriate
professional advice.